THE BUYERS GUIDE

AN ANALYSIS OF SELECTED U.S. POSTAGE STAMPS

STEPHEN R. DATZ

GENERAL PHILATELIC CORPORATION

LOVELAND, COLORADO

Printing History
First printing: April 1992
Second printing: March 1994

ISBN: 0-88219-026-1

Cover art: Mike Jenson

Manufactured in the United States of America

Published by General Philatelic Corporation
Post Office Box 402
Loveland, Colorado 80539

Acknowledgements

Writing a book is never an easy task. Without the generous assistance of George Brett, Richard A. Champagne, Walter Mader, Dr. Roberto Rosende, Jacques C. Schiff Jr., and Charles Shreve, this book would not have been a reality. I am grateful to them for finding the time to read the preliminary draft and for offering comments, criticisms, suggestions, and advice. I am especially indebted to Richard A. Champagne and Walter Mader, who were never too busy to take phone calls, answer questions, clarify details, or share their knowledge.

I don't know what I would have done without Andrea Rieger Datz's help. She spent countless hours over a period of many months diligently compiling stamp auction statistics.

And thanks to wife Susan for her suggestions, advice, and endless patience.

INTRODUCTION

The purpose of this book is to provide information about the qualitative characteristics of selected U.S. stamps. It is not intended to be an identification guide or a price guide. It is designed to be used as a spot reference, a convenient way to quickly check the individual characteristics of any random stamp. If read from cover to cover textbook-fashion, some information may appear to be redundant.

Stamps were selected based on value and rarity. Typically, stamps worth less than $100 each are not included separately, but sometimes appear as part of a set or series. Do not regard the omission of a stamp as a reflection on its desirability or worthiness; it was just not possible to include everything.

The commentary is divided into four sections: scarcity, comments, premium characteristics, and caveats.

SCARCITY

Quantity Issued. The number of stamps printed or issued according to government figures. The abbreviation *n/a* indicates that information about the quantity was not available. The abbreviation *est.* indicates that the figure given is an estimate.

Average Number At Auction. The total number of unused (or used) stamps divided by the number of auctions surveyed. The result is expressed as either a whole number or a fraction. For example, the number "2" indicates that on average, two copies of the stamp appeared at every auction. A fraction such as ".25" indicates that the stamp appeared only 25 time in 100 auctions, or one of every four auctions. The fraction ".02" indicates that the stamp appeared only two times in 100 auctions, or once every 50 auctions. The smaller the fraction, the less frequently the stamp appeared at auction.

Quantity issued is not always a reliable indicator of scarcity. Some stamps were issued in large numbers, but appear only infrequently on the market. Others, such as the Zeppelins, which were issued in relatively small numbers and purchased almost exclusively by collectors, appear frequently on the market. The average number at auction is an additional tool, a basis for comparison, an indication of a stamp's actual relative abundance or scarcity.

Occasionally, an anomaly occurs. Many auctions have a $50 or $100 net minimum lot value. Typically, stamps whose value is near the minimum do not appear at auction unless they are superlative examples expected to bring a strong price. In such borderline cases, infrequency at auction may make an inexpensive stamp appear scarce, when, in fact, it is not.

The symbol ★ indicates unused; the symbol ⊙ indicates used. For purposes of the survey, the unused category includes all uncancelled stamps without regard to presence or condition of gum. Generally, used stamps cataloging less than $100 were not included in the survey. Where data for a used stamp is omitted, it was not surveyed.

HINGING

For certain stamps, the number of never hinged (NH) copies appearing at auction was surveyed. The result is expressed as a percentage. If the number of copies encountered was insufficient to provide a valid sample, no result is given. The description *never hinged* assumes original gum. All stamps that could not be described as never hinged were assumed to have been hinged, including stamps without gum, disturbed gum, regummed, etc.

Statistics for early stamps are not given because never hinged copies are virtually unknown; in many cases, even copies with full original gum are very scarce.

COMMENTS

This section contains comments about the specific characteristics of each issue: centering, gum, margins, color, faults, etc. In some cases, stamps are examined on a stamp-by-stamp basis; in others, a series is examined with only brief comments about individual stamps.

PREMIUM CHARACTERISTICS

The stamp market is becoming more quality conscious. Collectors want the best: the best gum, the best margins, the best centering, the best color, etc. The term *premium quality* is used to describe the highest, most desirable state of each of these individual elements. The sum of the elements—gum, margins, centering, color, freshness, etc.—determines the overall grade of a stamp and its value. In some cases, good gum is more difficult to locate than balanced margins, in others, the opposite is true. The degree of difficulty for each element varies from issue to issue.

A stamp need not possess all the premium attributes in order to be a premium quality stamp. *In fact, it is unusual to find all the premium characteristics in a single stamp.* It is virtually impossible to find a sound, large margined, perfectly centered, never hinged, post-office-fresh Scott No. 1. That doesn't mean that a sound, modestly centered, no-gum, average colored, unused Scott No. 1 isn't a premium stamp; it is. It's a premium copy because it's superior to most unused Scott No. 1s, and that's what the concept of premium quality is all about; stamps that exhibit the best qualities for their issue. In some cases, it is not too difficult to locate a premium copy—such as a nicely centered, never hinged, post-office-fresh $2.60 Zeppelin; in others—such as Scott No. 1—it is almost impossible.

The analysis of premium characteristics on a stamp-by-stamp basis is designed to help you know what to expect from each issue, to know when you can hold out for total perfection, and when you should be ready to compromise. Knowing the degree of difficulty of an issue's premium elements also assists you in calculating their value. And that skill will prove more and more useful because the demand for premium quality stamps is accelerating. Experienced, knowledgeable buyers—those with whom you will be competing for ownership of choice stamps—recognize the genuine scarcity of premium quality stamps, especially nineteenth century issues, and are increasingly willing to pay double, triple, or, in some cases, even ten times catalogue, for the truly one-in-a-thousand gem.

Figure 1. The size of margins varies from issue to issue.

Margins. Large margins are a premium attribute. The size of margins varies from issue to issue, as shown in Figure 1. There is almost no space between some stamps, such as the 3-cent 1851s and 1857s. Others, such as the parcel posts, are spaced well apart. At minimum, a stamp should have margins of at least normal size for the issue. Generally, the larger the margins—assuming they are balanced—the more desirable the stamp.

Figure 2. Normal size margins on the left, jumbo margins on the right.

Oversized margins are referred to as *jumbo* or *boardwalk* margins; they are typically few and far between.

Figure 3. Examples of centering.

Centering. The way in which the design is situated in relation to the margins. In Figure 3., the stamp on the left is poorly centered; the one on the right possesses balanced margins. Balanced margins are a premium attribute. The more balanced the margins, the more visually appealing and desirable the stamp. Early stamps are notoriously poorly centered; they should not be compared to modern stamps. Some nineteenth century stamps have almost no room between stamps, which results in perforations touching or cutting on at least one side. Take this into account when judging centering. And remember, it is not always possible to find the perfectly centered copy; many experienced collectors content themselves with a reasonably centered copy for the issue. Centering characteristics appear with each listing.

Gum. Original gum (as opposed to regummed), never hinged, hinged, disturbed, partial, or missing. Gum is graded according to the severity of hinging: never hinged, lightly hinged, heavily hinged, hinge remnant, or disturbed gum. As a rule, the earlier the stamp, the more severe the hinging. Collectors used to seeing the pristine gum of twentieth century stamps have come to expect the same quality on early stamps. Unfortunately, the gum on most nineteenth century stamps is either partially or completely missing, heavily hinged, or disturbed from hinge removal.

In the early days, gum was made up in batches and applied primitively by hand with brushes, giving uneven results from one job to the next. After aging more than a century and a half, it has often cracked, browned, or otherwise degraded, and looks nothing like the gum on twentieth century stamps, the gum we are so accustomed to seeing on premium quality stamps. When confronted with early original gum, some find it so unappealing, so different from what they're used to that they refuse to believe it is, in fact, original gum. Often they'll pass up a perfectly good copy in order to wait for a better copy, unaware that better copies seldom come along. One school of thought is that original gum used during the first 25 years of stamp manufacture is so ugly that it's presence is unimportant anyway. Auctions frequently publish the disclaimer "original gum is not to be expected on stamps before 1890," and it is well to bear that in mind. As you will see in the stamp-by-stamp analysis, nineteenth century stamps possessing original gum are scarce. And except for a few low denominations, never hinged copies are very rare.

Most unused nineteenth stamps have been hinged, often heavily. In the early days of philately, collectors mounted stamps using bits of selvedge or any other paper handy. They gave no thought to future dismounting. The result is disturbed gum. Even used stamps sometimes have globs of insoluble glue adhering to their backs. Early, non-peelable stamp hinges often disturbed gum as much as the old paper hinges. Peelable hinges left gum in better condition. Now, hinges are avoided altogether, and, increasingly, collectors want never hinged stamps.

As with centering, the goal is to find premium gum, measuring a stamp's attributes against others of its issue, not against modern issues. For early nineteenth century stamps the presence of any reasonably attractive gum—be it hinged or not—is a bonus. One must be very forgiving about the condition of gum on early issues. For later nineteenth century stamps it means, lightly hinged original gum or never hinged where possible. For many issues, lightly hinged is the best one can reasonably expect. Twentieth century issues are generally never hinged, although light hinging is more realistic for some the rare issues.

The survey revealed that only a minuscule percentage of expensive, key nineteenth century stamps are never hinged. Certification by a competent expertizing body is essential for expensive nineteenth century stamps purported to be never hinged.

Perforations. Reasonably intact perforations are a premium attribute. The ideal is to have perforations as balanced as possible *within the limits of the issue*. The majority of nineteenth century stamps exist with irregular perforations, which generally are not considered a fault.

Some issues, such as the hard paper banknotes, are prone to irregular perfs because they were printed on brittle paper with poor separation characteristics. The 1875 reprints of the 1857-60 issue usually exhibit ragged, irregular, or short perfs;

that's just the way they come. Others, such as perf 8½ or perf 10 issues, separate poorly due to the size or spacing of perforation holes. Sometimes perforating equipment did not completely punch out holes, leaving them filled with circular bits of paper. The condition of perfs must be viewed in context with what is usual for an issue. Where irregular perfs are the norm, they should not be considered a fault. Note the perforations in the illustrations appearing with each listing to get a better feel for each stamp's perf characteristics.

Short or pulled perfs—as opposed to irregular perfs—refers to perforation teeth that are missing, usually all the way to the base of the perf or below it. Short perfs are generally considered a minor fault, unless they are characteristic of an issue.

Color. How vivid or pronounced color is within the range of shades that exist. Usually, the more intense the color, the more appealing the stamp. Premium quality color should be as near to the issued state as possible. Adjectives such as fresh, bright, vivid, and intense are used to describe stamps with premium color characteristics. Some stamps, most notably orange colored, tend to discolor when they come in contact with sulphur compounds, either atmospheric or in album or stockbook papers. Others, such as Scott No. 71, are notoriously poorly colored, a condition mentioned where appropriate. Again, a stamp's color must be measured against others of its kind, not against other issues that are routinely boldly colored.

Freshness. How near to the original post office state the stamp is. Ideally, a stamp possesses "mint bloom" and pristine paper. Stamps turned brownish or yellowish from albums or stockbooks made of cheap paper are visually unappealing and avoided by knowledgeable buyers.

Cancels. The ideal cancel is neat, clear and does not distract from or obliterate the underlying design of the stamp. It is legitimate and contemporaneous to the stamp. Serious collectors avoid favor cancels or contrived cancels, especially on expensive stamps—such as Scott Nos. 459, 491, 539, etc.—whose used value is about the same as their unused value. Stamps of this type are often seen with bogus cancels because clean used copies are more salable than no-gum or heavily hinged unused copies.

Colored and specialty cancels can be worth considerable premiums, especially on early stamps. Pen cancels detract from the value of many early stamps. Refer to the *Scott Specialized Catalogue* for specific information on varieties and prices.

Faults. Major faults include tears, thins, pinholes, creases, scuffs, abrasions, stains, foxing, discolorations, and glazed or tropicalized gum. Minor or trivial faults include such things as perf bends and perf thins. *The vast majority of nineteenth century stamps are faulty.* The earlier the stamp, the greater the percentage of its population will be faulty.

Sometimes stamps with faults are "improved": creases ironed out; discolorations bleached; pinholes and thins filled; small scuffs and abrasions carefully colored to match original ink and disguise the fault. Often faults or improvements are not obvious; it is prudent to check stamps carefully for any sign of tampering. This cannot be stressed strongly enough. The presence of a major fault generally diminishes the value of a stamp substantially. However, that is not the case for extremely rare stamps that almost always contain faults.

Natural inclusions (material embedded in paper during its manufacture), unnaturally irregular perfs, gum skips, perf dimples, toned paper, natural gum skips, and natural gum bends (unless severe enough to have broken the paper fibers), while not technically faults, are elements often avoided by demanding buyers. The absence of these elements generally enhances the value of a stamp.

The Sum of Elements. As we've said, depending on the issue, some premium elements are more difficult than others. For example, it is easier to find never hinged Washington-Franklins than nicely centered ones. Finding the best of both elements in a single stamp is much more difficult than finding either individual attribute. Suppose one in ten stamps is never hinged, and one in twenty is well centered. Using the mathematics of probability, one might conclude that number of stamps possessing both qualities would be one in two hundred (one in ten times twenty). And the more elements that are added to the equation, the more difficult the outcome. Bear this in mind when looking for the ideal stamp, the stamp that is sound, beautifully centered, large margined, never hinged, and pristinely colored.

One more thing—maintain a sense of balance. Never let the quest for quality blind you to the limitations of an issue. Some buyers become so obsessed with quality that they begin to find something wrong with every stamp, regardless of its general excellence. Avoid unrealistic expectations, and never forget the frailties and limitations of nineteenth century stamps.

Rarity. As mentioned, the rarer the stamp, the more difficult it will be to find in premium condition. Some stamps are so rare that a reasonable population of candidates simply does not exist, and selectivity, in the normal sense, is not possible.

CAVEATS

Comments intended to alert buyers to potential problems. Caveats are directed more toward the collector than the dealer, who is presumed to be more knowledgeable about the dangers inherent in various issues.

Regumming and Reperfing. Regumming and reperfing are facts of life. The art of regumming has become more sophisticated over the years, until at present, skilled jobs are difficult to detect except by professionals who handle stamps every day. Buyers should be aware of the risk, but not intimidated by it. Despite the growing sophistication of stamp "mechanics," most regumming jobs are easy to spot if you know what to look for. *How to Detect Damaged, Altered, and Repaired Stamps,* by Paul Schmid, is one of the best general books on the subject. Every serious collector should own a copy.

All nineteenth century stamps should be examined for reperfing, and, if unused, for regumming, especially if offered as never hinged. Be extremely cautious of expensive stamps, especially high values of the Columbian and Trans-Mississippi series. In examining collections over the years, I have found that the vast majority of so-called never hinged nineteenth century stamps had, in fact, been regummed. Some regummed stamps have even been lightly hinged to throw buyers off guard. Buy from reliable sources, dealers who have been in business for a number of years and who have a reputation for integrity. Learn to spot signs of tampering, or, if not, know when it is appropriate to submit a stamp for an expert opinion.

Fakes. Buyers are cautioned about fakes where appropriate. Dangerous fakes of some stamps exist, and in the case of Washington-Franklin coils, they are endemic. Faking is nothing new. Many fakes were made decades ago, so the fact that a stamp has been in a collection for 50 years has little bearing on its genuineness.

Expert Certificates. Expert certificates are advised in many cases, sometimes for authenticity of the stamp, sometimes for gum, sometimes for use on cover.

Certificate recommended indicates a moderate degree of risk. A certificate may not be necessary for dealers or those with experience handling the stamps in question.

Certificate strongly recommended indicates a greater degree of risk. Those without the expertise to recognize the problems inherent in such stamps should get an expert opinion.

Certificate essential indicates a high degree of risk. These stamps should be certified regardless of your level of expertise.

METHODOLOGY

One hundred auctions were surveyed to gather statistics for *Average Number Appearing at Auction* and for *NH vs. Hinged.* Cumulatively, the auctions contained over 100,000 lots, including more than 25,000 lots featuring stamps used in this guide. The auctions are listed in the bibliography.

For certain sets (such as the Panama Pacific issue), only the top value or most expensive value was surveyed. Typical condition for other values in such sets can be inferred from general comments about the surveyed stamp.

The statistics are not intended to be a definitive census of surviving copies, but rather a sample of sufficient proportion to give a general picture of relative scarcity, hinging, etc. *It is our impression that it is the best copies that usually surface at auction, therefore, one may assume that the results of the survey are skewed toward a greater number of high quality, never hinged stamps than actually exists.*

A FINAL NOTE

Nothing substitutes for experience. Look at as many stamps as you can—at dealers, at clubs, at stamp shows, and in auction catalogues. Take time to familiarize yourself with their characteristics. And don't be afraid to ask questions. The more you know about the characteristics of each issue, the better you will be able to appreciate the scarceness of a truly premium copy, and the more comfortable you will be when the question of price and value arises.

It's been said that philately is largely based on aesthetics, on eye appeal. The concept of premium quality, too, is rooted in aesthetics. Each of us knows a lovely stamp when we see it. So in the final analysis, it all boils down to a matter of subjective judgement and price. If this book has helped familiarize you the characteristics of individual issues and enabled you to better gauge their value, it will have accomplished its purpose.

5c BROWN
YEAR OF ISSUE: 1847
SCOTT NO. 1

Scarcity
Quantity Issued: 3,700,000
★ Average No./Auction: .54
⊙ Average No./Auction: 5.00

Comments
Copies often display an indistinct appearance, a lack of crispness. The range varies from relatively pronounced color and impression to weak, very low contrast copies. Generally, the more visually appealing the impression and color, the more desirable the stamp. Without some experience, it is very difficult to judge the merits of an isolated individual example. Typically, an inexperienced buyer's impression on seeing their first No. 1

is that something's wrong with the stamp because its appearance tends to be so drab. No. 1s also exist in a wonderful variety of shades ranging from deep walnut through browns, red browns, and orange browns. Just remember that No. 1's charms are subtle. The stamp's appearance is often enhanced by a variety of colored and specialty cancels, some of which command a substantial premium. The red grid cancel is the most common. Pen canceled copies are considered less desirable and sell for about half.

Due to narrow spacing, large-margined copies are scarce. Full original gum should not be expected on unused copies; never hinged examples are exceedingly rare. Faults are commonplace, especially minor ones such as corner creases.

Premium Characteristics
Sound copy with four large, balanced margins, crisp impression (within the limits of the issue), good color (again, within the limits of the issue); neat, clear device cancel, if used. Premium unused copies are rare; premium used copies are somewhat scarce.

Caveats
Beware ironed-out creases, pin-holes, minor defects, and repairs. Beware chemically cleaned used copies passing for unused. Beware fake grid or other cancellations concealing removed pen cancels. Certificate strongly recommended for unused copies, shades, and expensive cancel varieties.

An array of 4-margin copies. Note the variation in printing impression, size of margins, and cancellations. The copy at the top of the page is about as nice as they come.

10c BLACK
YEAR OF ISSUE: 1847
SCOTT NO. 2

Scarcity
Quantity Issued: 865,000
★ Average No./Auction: .22
⊙ Average No./Auction: 4.32

Comments
Engraved impression much sharper than the 5-cent 1847. Due to narrow spacing, large margined copies are scarce. The larger the margins, the

more eye-appealing the stamp. A variety of colored and specialty cancels exist, some of which command a substantial premium. The red grid cancel is the most common; together with the black color of the stamp, they form a handsome combination. Pen canceled copies are considered less desirable and sell for about half.

Full original gum should not be expected on unused copies; never hinged examples are exceedingly rare.

Premium Characteristics
Four large, balanced margins; neat, clear device cancel, if used. Premium unused copies are very rare; premium used copies are somewhat scarce.

Caveats
Beware ironed-out creases, pin-holes, minor defects, and repairs; they are commonplace. Beware chemically cleaned used copies passing for unused. Beware fake grid or other cancellations concealing removed pen cancels. Certificate essential for unused copies and for copies with expensive cancel varieties.

An array of 4-margin copies. Note the variation—which is typical—in the size of margins and in the cancellations. The illustrated copies are of reasonable quality and better than many, which often lack four margins or contain crooked scissors cuts that are visually unattractive. The large copy at the top of the page is a gem, possessing large, nicely balanced margins and a neat cancel. Expect to pay a premium for that kind of quality.

5c RED BROWN
YEAR OF ISSUE: 1875
SCOTT NO. 3

Scarcity
Quantity Issued: 4,779
★ Average No./Auction: .93

Comments
Colors range from weak browns to rich orange browns. Engraved impression generally sharper than the 5-cent 1847. Issued without gum. Typically, more nicely margined than the 1847 issue. Not valid for postage, however, used copies are known.

Premium Characteristics
Four large, balanced margins, fresh color. Premium copies are not scarce.

Caveats
Beware ironed-out creases, minor defects, and repairs. Beware India proofs passing as stamps. Although faults are not as commonplace on this issue as on the 1847 issue, about one-third the copies surveyed were faulty.

10c BLACK
YEAR OF ISSUE: 1875
SCOTT NO. 4

Scarcity
Quantity Issued: 3,883
★ Average No./Auction: .82

Comments
Typically, more nicely margined than the 1847 issue. Issued without gum. Not valid for postage, however, used copies are known.

Premium Characteristics
Four large, balanced margins, fresh color. Premium copies are not rare.

Caveats
Beware ironed-out creases, minor defects, and repairs. Beware India proofs passing as stamps. Although faults are not as commonplace on this issue as on the 1847 issue, about one-third the copies surveyed were faulty.

An array of 4-margin copies typical of those commonly encountered.

1c BLUE, Type I
YEAR OF ISSUE: 1851
SCOTT NO. 5

Scarcity
Quantity Issued: very rare

Comments
A great rarity. Most copies are faulty. Seldom comes to market. Because of its extreme rarity, each example stands on its own merits.

Caveats
Certificate essential.

The design is typically cut on one or more sides. Compared to other 1-cent 1851 types, color is lighter, often referred to as "powder" blue, and printing impression less crisp. The vast majority contain faults. Original gum should not be expected on unused copies. In fact, copies with original gum are rare, and never hinged examples are virtually nonexistent. Nicely pen cancelled copies are acceptable and sell for about 66-75 percent of device cancelled copies.

1c BLUE, Type Ib
YEAR OF ISSUE: 1851
SCOTT NO. 5A

Scarcity
Quantity Issued: rare
★ Average No./Auction: .06
☉ Average No./Auction: .13

Comments
Narrow spacing between stamps, especially top and bottom, makes fully margined copies very difficult.

Premium Characteristics
Sound, four complete margins (within the limits of the issue); neat, clear cancel of the period, if used. Premium copies are rare. Positions 6R1E and 8R1E command a premium of approximately 50 percent.

Caveats
Beware ironed-out creases, minor defects, and repairs. Top and bottom margins must be clear and uncovered by cancels in order to positively identify this type. Certificate essential.

Some examples of the 1-cent 1851 (illustration includes various types and is intended only to give an idea of typical margins and scissors cuts). The illustrated examples are about as nice as one can reasonably expect to find.

1c BLUE, Type Ia
YEAR OF ISSUE: 1851
SCOTT NO. 6

Scarcity
Quantity Issued: rare
★ Average No./Auction: .04
☺ Average No./Auction: .28

Comments
Same general comments that apply to Scott No. 5A.

Premium Characteristics
Sound, four complete margins (within the limits of the issue); neat, clear cancels of the period, if used copies. Premium copies are rare. The illustrated example is a gem, a copy as nice as they come.

Caveats
Beware ironed-out creases, minor defects, and repairs. It is vital that copies show full bottom scrolls, therefore, top and bottom margins must be clear and uncovered by cancels in order to positively identify this type. Beware stamps faked by the addition of certain engraved lines to simulate Type Ia. Certificate essential.

1c BLUE, Type III
YEAR OF ISSUE: 1851
SCOTT NO. 8

Scarcity
Quantity Issued: rare
★ Average No./Auction: .05
☺ Average No./Auction: .32

Comments
Narrow spacing between stamps, especially top and bottom, makes fully margined copies very difficult. The design is typically cut on one or more sides. Copies with wide breaks in the outer lines (¼" top and bottom) are worth much more than those with smaller breaks. The vast majority contain faults. Original gum should not be expected. In fact, copies with original gum are rare; never hinged examples are virtually nonexistent. Colored cancellations are worth a premium. Nicely pen cancelled copies are acceptable and sell for about 66-75 percent of device cancelled copies.

Premium Characteristics
Sound, four complete margins (within the limits of the issue); neat, clear cancels of the period, if used. Clear, wide breaks both top and bottom. Premium copies are rare. The illustrated example is a gem, as nice a copy as you could hope to find.

Caveats
Beware occasional fakes made from perforated copies. Beware widened breaks created by erasure. Beware ironed-out creases, minor defects, and repairs. Certificate essential.

1c BLUE, Type IIIa
YEAR OF ISSUE: 1851
SCOTT NO. 8A

Scarcity
Quantity Issued: rare
★ Average No./Auction: .09
⊙ Average No./Auction: .60

Comments
Narrow spacing between stamps,

especially top and bottom, makes fully margined copies very difficult. The design is typically cut on one or more sides. This stamp is usually faulty. Original gum should not be expected on unused copies; never hinged examples are extremely scarce. Colored cancellations are worth a premium. Pen canceled copies sell for about half.

Premium Characteristics
Sound condition, four complete margins (within the limits of the issue); neat, clear cancels of the period, if used. Premium copies are very scarce. The illustrated example is a gem of uncommonly high quality.

Caveats
Beware occasional fakes made from perforated copies. Beware ironed-out creases, minor defects, and repairs. Certificate essential.

1c BLUE, Type IV
YEAR OF ISSUE: 1851
SCOTT NO. 9

Scarcity
Quantity Issued: scarce
★ Average No./Auction: .57
⊙ Average No./Auction: 1.30

Comments
Narrow spacing between stamps,

especially top and bottom, makes fully margined copies very difficult. The design is typically cut on one or more sides. This stamp is often faulty. Original gum should not be expected on unused copies; never hinged examples are scarce. Colored cancellations are worth a premium. Pen canceled copies sell for about half. Stamps with top or bottom lines trimmed away sell at substantial discounts. Several of the recutting varieties are scarce and command a premium.

Premium Characteristics
Sound condition, four complete margins (within the limits of the issue); neat, clear cancel of the period, if used. Premium unused copies are rare; premium used copies are more easily obtainable. The illustrated example is a beautifully margined unused copy.

Caveats
Beware ironed-out creases, minor defects, and repairs. Certificate recommended.

3c ORANGE BROWN, Type I
YEAR OF ISSUE: 1851
SCOTT NO. 10

Scarcity
Quantity Issued: rare
★ Average No./Auction: .22
⊚ Average No./Auction: .23

Comments
Extremely narrow spacing between

stamps makes fully margined copies difficult. Note the spacing between stamps at the top of the illustration. About than half the copies surveyed were faulty. Original gum should not be expected on unused copies; never hinged examples, if they exist, are exceedingly rare. Exists in a number of shades of which the copper brown and deep orange brown are very desirable. A variety of colored and specialty cancels exists, many of which are scarce and worth a premium. Pen canceled copies sell for about sixty percent.

Premium Characteristics
Sound condition, four complete margins, if possible (unused four margin copies are exceedingly rare); neat, clear cancel of the period, if used. Premium copies are difficult. The illustrated example is a gem.

Caveats
Beware ironed-out creases, minor defects, and repairs. Certificate essential for unused copies and expensive specialty cancels.

5c RED BROWN, Type I
YEAR OF ISSUE: 1856
SCOTT NO. 12

Scarcity
Quantity Issued: rare
★ Average No./Auction: .22
⊚ Average No./Auction: 1.88

Comments
Narrow spacing between stamps

makes fully margined copies difficult. More than half the copies surveyed were faulty. Original gum should not be expected on unused copies; never hinged examples exist but are exceedingly rare. Colored cancels are prized and worth a premium. Pen canceled copies sell for about half.

Premium Characteristics
Sound condition, four complete margins; neat, clear cancel of the period, if used. Large margins are especially desirable. Premium copies are scarce. The illustrated example is a gem.

Caveats
Beware fakes made from perforated copies of the less expensive Scott No. 28 or Scott No. 29, which is brown rather than red brown. Beware ironed-out creases, minor defects, and repairs. Beware proofs of the same or nearly same color passing for unused stamps. Certificate essential for unused copies, and recommended for used copies.

10c GREEN, Type I
YEAR OF ISSUE: 1855
SCOTT NO. 13

Scarcity
Quantity Issued: rare
★ Average No./Auction: .14
⊙ Average No./Auction: 1.10

Comments
Spacing between stamps somewhat wider than other values of this series;

margins clear of the design are less difficult. Still, the design is often cut on one or more sides. More than half the copies surveyed were faulty. Original gum should not be expected on unused copies; never hinged examples are virtually nonexistent. Pen canceled copies sell for half or less.

Premium Characteristics
Sound condition, four large, balanced margins; neat, clear cancels of the period, if used. Premium copies scarce. The illustrated example is a premium quality copy.

Caveats
Beware fakes made from perforated copies of Scott No. 35. Beware ironed-out creases, minor defects, and repairs, including regumming and cleaned cancels. Certificate essential for unused copies, and recommended for used copies.

10c GREEN, Type II
YEAR OF ISSUE: 1856
SCOTT NO. 14

Scarcity
Quantity Issued: n/a
★ Average No./Auction: .26
⊙ Average No./Auction: 1.10

Comments
Spacing between stamps somewhat wider than other values of this series; margins clear of the design are less difficult. Still, the design is often cut on one or more sides. Original gum should not be expected on unused copies; never hinged examples are

virtually nonexistent. Pen canceled copies sell for about half. About half the copies surveyed were faulty.

Premium Characteristics
Sound condition, four large, balanced margins; free of faults; neat, clear cancel of the period, if used. Premium copies are scarce.

Caveats
Beware fakes made from perforated copies of Scott No. 35. Beware ironed-out creases, minor defects, and repairs, including regumming and cleaned cancels. Certificate essential for unused copies and recommended for used copies.

A word about stamps of the 1851-1857 issues: a stamp's color should be strong; the engraved impression clear; the type, if relevant, obvious; the cancel neat, clear, and of the period contemporary to the stamp. Pen cancellations are sometimes chemically removed and device cancels (grids, circular date cancels, colored or specialty cancels, etc.) added to improve the value of the stamp. It is prudent to have any stamp with a cancel that substantially increases its value expertised.

10c GREEN, Type III
YEAR OF ISSUE: 1855
SCOTT NO. 15

Scarcity
Quantity Issued: scarce
★ Average No./Auction: .26
☉ Average No./Auction: 2.63

Comments
Spacing between stamps somewhat wider than other values of this series; margins clear of the design are less difficult. Still, the design is often cut on one or more sides. Faults are commonplace. Original gum should not be expected on unused copies; never hinged examples are virtually nonexistent. Pen canceled copies sell for half or less.

Premium Characteristics
Sound condition, four large, balanced margins; neat, clear cancel of the period, if used. Premium copies are scarce.

Caveats
Beware fakes made from perforated copies of Scott No. 35. Beware ironed-out creases, minor defects, and repairs, including regumming and cleaned cancels. Certificate essential for unused copies and recommended for used copies.

10c GREEN, Type IV
YEAR OF ISSUE: 1856
SCOTT NO. 16

Scarcity
Quantity Issued: rare
★ Average No./Auction: .05
☉ Average No./Auction: .76

Comments
Unused this is one of the rarest of nineteenth century stamps. Spacing between stamps somewhat wider than other values of this series, making larger margins more common. Still, the design is often cut on one or more sides. Faults are commonplace. Original gum should not be expected on unused copies; never hinged examples are virtually nonexistent. Pen canceled copies sell for about half.

Premium Characteristics
Because of its great rarity, it is unrealistic to hold this stamp to the same standard that normally applies to premium copies. More than 80 percent of the unused copies encountered in the survey contained faults, therefore, each copy must stand on its own merits. Sound condition, four balanced margins; free of faults; neat, clear cancel of the period for used copies. Clear impression of re-cut lines is desirable, especially the variety re-cut at both top and bottom. Premium copies are scarce.

Caveats
Beware fakes made from perforated copies of Scott No. 35. Beware fakes created from Types II or III. Beware ironed-out creases, minor defects, and repairs, including regumming and cleaned cancels. Certificate essential for unused copies and recommended for used copies.

An array of 10-cent greens illustrating typical scissors cuts and centering.

12c BLACK
YEAR OF ISSUE: 1851
SCOTT NO. 17

Scarcity
Quantity Issued: n/a
★ Average No./Auction: .35
⊚ Average No./Auction: 1.74

Comments
Spacing between stamps is extremely narrow. Design is typically cut on one or more sides. Faults are commonplace. Original gum should not be expected on unused copies; never hinged examples are extremely rare. Pen canceled copies sell for half or less. Colored and specialty cancels command a premium.

Premium Characteristics
Sound condition, four complete margins; neat, clear cancel of the period, if used. Premium copies are scarce.

Caveats
Beware ironed-out creases, minor defects, and repairs, including regumming and cleaned cancels. Beware fakes created from perforated copies. Certificate essential for unused copies and recommended for used copies.

1c BLUE, Type I
YEAR OF ISSUE: 1857
SCOTT NO. 18

Scarcity
Quantity Issued: scarce
★ Average No./Auction: .28
⊚ Average No./Auction: .42

Comments
Spacing between stamps is very narrow. Perforations usually touch or cut on one or more sides. Touching or cutting perfs should not be considered a fault. Copies usually have a bluish cast, referred to as plate wash, which is not a fault and is often described as typical Type I color. Original gum should not be expected on unused copies, however, it is more commonly encountered on Scott No. 18 than on other 1-cent 1857s. Never hinged examples exist but are rare. Faults are commonplace. Pen canceled copies sell for about half.

Premium Characteristics
Sound condition, reasonably balanced margins (within the limits of the issue); neat, clear cancel of the period, if used. Copies showing full design at the bottom are preferred. Premium copies are very scarce. The illustrated example is a gem.

Caveats
Beware ironed-out creases, small tears, minor defects, and repairs, including reperfing, added perfs, and regumming. Beware proofs perforated to simulate stamps. Beware design characteristics added to simulate Type I. Color varies in intensity and is susceptible to cleaning. Certificate recommended, especially for unused copies

1c BLUE, Type Ia
YEAR OF ISSUE: 1857
SCOTT NO. 19

Scarcity
Quantity Issued: rare
★ Average No./Auction: .03
⊙ Average No./Auction: .16

Comments
Characteristically, a deep, rich shade of blue. Vertical spacing between stamps is extremely narrow. Design is typically cut on one or more sides. Touching or cutting perfs are not considered a fault. Must have the "F" relief flaw to be a genuine example. Original gum should not be expected on unused copies; never hinged examples, if they exist, are exceedingly rare. Faults are commonplace. Pen canceled copies sell for 50-80 percent, depending on the premium characteristics of the underlying stamp. Colored and specialty cancels command a premium. This stamp is very rare; selectivity in the normal sense is not possible.

Premium Characteristics
Reasonably balanced margins within the limits of the issue; free of faults; neat, clear cancel of the period for used copies. Premium copies are very rare and command a substantial premium.

Caveats
Beware ironed-out creases, minor defects, and repairs, including reperfing and regumming. Color varies in intensity and is susceptible to cleaning. Certificate recommended, especially for unused copies.

1c BLUE, Type II
YEAR OF ISSUE: 1857
SCOTT NO. 20

Scarcity
Quantity Issued: n/a
★ Average No./Auction: .28
⊙ Average No./Auction: .37

Comments
Vertical spacing between stamps is extremely narrow. Perforations usually touch or cut on one or more sides. Touching or cutting perfs should not be considered a fault. Original gum should not be expected on unused copies; never hinged examples exist but are scarce.

Original gum copies from plate 11 are more often encountered than from plates 2 or 4. Examples from plate 11 typically exhibit plate wash. Faults are commonplace. Pen canceled copies sell for about 40 percent.

Premium Characteristics
Sound condition, reasonably balanced margins (within the limits of the issue); neat, clear cancel of the period for used copies. Premium copies are very scarce.

Caveats
Beware ironed-out creases, minor defects, and repairs, including reperfing and regumming. Color varies in intensity and is susceptible to cleaning. Certificate recommended, especially for unused copies.

Note the tight margins and how perforations typically touch or cut the design.

1c BLUE, Type III
YEAR OF ISSUE: 1857
SCOTT NO. 21

Scarcity
Quantity Issued: very scarce
★ Average No./Auction: .20
⊙ Average No./Auction: .32

Comments
Spacing between stamps is extremely narrow. Perforations typically touch

or cut on one or more sides and are not considered a fault. Wide breaks at top and bottom show the type clearly and command a substantial premium. Original gum should not be expected on unused copies; never hinged examples are rare. Faults are commonplace. Pen canceled copies sell for half. Colored and specialty cancels command a premium.

Premium Characteristics
Sound condition, reasonably balanced margins (within the limits of the issue); neat, clear cancel of the period for used copies. Premium copies are rare. The illustrated copy is as nice as one could hope to find, and very rare at that.

Caveats
Beware copies of Scott No. 24 with side ornaments drawn in to resemble Scott No. 21. Beware ironed-out creases, minor defects, and repairs, including reperfing and regumming. Color varies in intensity and is susceptible to cleaning. Certificate recommended, especially for unused copies.

1c BLUE, Type IIIa
YEAR OF ISSUE: 1857
SCOTT NO. 22

Scarcity
Quantity Issued: very scarce
★ Average No./Auction: .20
⊙ Average No./Auction: .32

Comments
This stamp is scarcer than Scott No.

20. Spacing between stamps is extremely narrow. Perforations typically touch or cut on one or more sides and are not considered a fault. Original gum should not be expected on unused copies; never hinged examples are rare. Half the copies surveyed were faulty. Pen canceled copies sell for half. Colored and specialty cancels command a premium.

Premium Characteristics
Reasonably balanced margins (within the limits of the issue); free of faults; neat, clear cancel of the period, if used. Premium copies are rare and very difficult. The illustrated example is as nice a copy as one is likely to encounter.

Caveats
Beware ironed-out creases, minor defects, and repairs, including reperfing and regumming. Color varies in intensity and is susceptible to cleaning. Certificate recommended, especially for unused copies.

1c BLUE, Type IV
YEAR OF ISSUE: 1857
SCOTT NO. 23

Scarcity
Quantity Issued: rare
★ Average No./Auction: .07
◉ Average No./Auction: .33

Comments
Spacing between stamps is extremely narrow. Perforations usually touch or cut on one or more sides and are not considered a fault. Original gum should not be expected on unused copies; never hinged examples are exceedingly rare. Faults are commonplace. Pen canceled copies sell for half. Colored and specialty cancels command a premium.

Premium Characteristics
Reasonably balanced margins (within the limits of the issue); free of faults; neat, clear cancel of the period, if used. Premium copies are rare. The illustrated example is a gem of much higher quality than usually encountered.

Caveats
Beware ironed-out creases, minor defects, and repairs, including reperfing and regumming. Beware fakes made by perforating the more common Scott No. 9. Color varies in intensity and is susceptible to cleaning. Certificate recommended, especially for unused copies.

1c BLUE, Type V
YEAR OF ISSUE: 1857
SCOTT NO. 24

Scarcity
Quantity Issued: n/a
★ Average No./Auction: .39

Comments
This stamp is the most common of the 1857 1-cent types. Spacing between stamps is extremely narrow. Perforations usually touch or cut on one or more sides and are not considered a fault. Original gum should not be expected on unused copies; never hinged examples are scarce. Faults are commonplace. Pen canceled copies sell for half. Colored and specialty cancels command a premium.

Premium Characteristics
Sound condition, balanced margins with perforations clear of the design (balanced jumbo margins command a substantial premium); neat, clear cancel of the period for used copies. Premium unused copies are fairly difficult. The illustrated example is a magnificent unused copy.

Caveats
Beware ironed-out creases, minor defects, and repairs, including reperfing and regumming. Color varies in intensity and is susceptible to cleaning. Certificate recommended for unused premium copies or used copies with expensive cancels.

3c ROSE, Type I
YEAR OF ISSUE: 1857
SCOTT NO. 25

Scarcity
Quantity Issued: scarce
★ Average No./Auction: .24

Comments
Spacing between stamps is extremely narrow. Perforations usually touch or cut on one or more sides. Irregular perfs are typical and not considered a fault. Original gum should not be expected on unused copies; never hinged examples are very scarce. Faults are commonplace. Pen canceled copies sell for about half. Colored and specialty cancels command a premium (many substantial).

Premium Characteristics
Sound condition, reasonably centered (within the limits of the issue); neat, clear cancel of the period, if used. Premium unused copies are scarce; premium used copies are not difficult. The illustrated unused example is a gem as nice as they come. Note the extreme tightness of margins and the irregular perfs.

Caveats
Beware ironed-out creases, minor defects, removed cancels, and repairs, including reperfing and regumming. Certificate recommended for unused copies.

3c ROSE, Type II
YEAR OF ISSUE: 1857
SCOTT NO. 26

Scarcity
Quantity Issued: n/a
★ Average No./Auction: .32

Note. This stamp is relatively inexpensive and, therefore, infrequently offered at auction because it usually does not qualify for the minimum lot value. The unused copies that did appear at auction were of superior quality. Used copies were not surveyed.

Comments
Spacing between stamps is extremely narrow. Perforations usually touch or cut on one or more sides. Irregular perfs are typical and not considered a fault. Original gum should not be expected on unused copies; never hinged examples are scarce. Faults are commonplace. Pen canceled copies sell for less. Colored and specialty cancels command a premium (many substantial).

Premium Characteristics
Sound condition, reasonably centered (within the limits of the issue); lightly hinged or never hinged original gum; neat, clear cancel of the period, if used. Premium unused copies are available, but not abundant. Premium used copies are not difficult.

Caveats
Beware ironed-out creases, minor defects, removed cancels, and repairs, including reperfing and regumming. Certificate recommended for unused premium copies and used copies with expensive cancels.

3c DULL RED, Type IIa
YEAR OF ISSUE: 1857
SCOTT NO. 26a

Scarcity
Quantity Issued: n/a
★ Average No./Auction: .03

Comments
This stamp is much scarcer than its predecessor (Scott No. 26), especially unused. Spacing between stamps is extremely narrow. Perforations usually touch or cut on one or more sides. Irregular perfs are typical and not considered a fault. Original gum should not be expected on unused copies; never hinged examples are rare. Faults are commonplace. Pen canceled copies sell for about half. Colored and specialty cancels command a premium (many substantial).

Premium Characteristics
Sound condition, reasonably centered (within the limits of the issue); original gum; neat, clear cancel of the period, if used. Premium unused copies are very difficult; premium used copies are available, but scarce.

Caveats
Beware ironed-out creases, minor defects, removed cancels, and repairs, including reperfing and regumming. Certificate recommended for unused copies and used copies with expensive cancels.

5c BRICK RED, Type I
YEAR OF ISSUE: 1858
SCOTT NO. 27

Scarcity
Quantity Issued: n/a
★ Average No./Auction: .10
⊙ Average No./Auction: .85

Comments
Spacing between stamps is narrow. Perforations usually touch or cut on one or more sides. Touching or cutting perfs should not be considered a fault. In fact, copies with perfs clear of the design are almost impossible to find. Color typically appears pale or washed out compared to subsequent issues. Unused copies are rare. Original gum should not be expected on unused copies; never hinged examples are virtually unknown. Faults are commonplace. Pen canceled copies sell for about half. Only one unused block of 4 is known.

Premium Characteristics
Sound condition, reasonably balanced margins; neat, clear cancel of the period, if used. Premium unused copies are extremely rare; premium used copies are scarce. Note the narrowness of the margins and condition of the perfs on the illustrated example, which is a gem.

Caveats
Beware ironed-out creases, minor defects, and repairs, including reperfing and regumming. Certificate essential for unused copies and recommended for used copies.

5c RED BROWN, Type I
YEAR OF ISSUE: 1857
SCOTT NO. 28

Scarcity
Quantity Issued: scarce
★ Average No./Auction: .10
⊘ Average No./Auction: .38

Comments
This is a scarce stamp, appearing much less frequently at auction than Scott No. 27. It occurs in many interesting shades. Spacing between stamps is narrow. Perforations usually touch or cut on one or more sides. Touching or cutting perfs should not be considered a fault. Unused copies are scarce. Original gum should not be expected on unused copies; never hinged examples are extremely rare. Faults are commonplace. Pen canceled copies sell for about half.

Premium Characteristics
Sound condition, bold color, reasonably balanced margins (perfs clear of the design are a bonus); neat, clear cancel of the period, if used. Premium unused copies are rare; premium used copies are scarce.

Caveats
Beware ironed-out creases, minor defects, and repairs, including reperfing and regumming. Certificate essential for unused copies and strongly recommended for used copies.

5c INDIAN RED, Type I
YEAR OF ISSUE: 1858
SCOTT NO. 28A

Scarcity
Quantity Issued: rare
★ Average No./Auction: .02
⊘ Average No./Auction: .18

Comments
A very rare stamp, and one of the most misidentified nineteenth century issues. Spacing between stamps is narrow. Perforations usually touch or cut on one or more sides. Touching or cutting perfs should not be considered a fault. Irregular perfs are typical and are not considered a fault. Unused copies are very rare.

Original gum should not be expected on unused copies. Faults are commonplace. Pen canceled copies sell for about seventy percent.

Premium Characteristics
Sound condition, bold color, balanced margins (perfs clear of the design are a bonus); neat, clear cancel of the period, if used. Premium unused copies are exceedingly rare; selectivity in the normal sense is not possible. Premium used copies are quite scarce.

Caveats
Beware ironed-out creases, minor defects, and repairs, including reperfing and regumming. Certificate essential.

Examples of 5-cent 1857s. Note tight margins and typical irregular perfs.

5c BROWN, Type I
YEAR OF ISSUE: 1859
SCOTT NO. 29

Scarcity
Quantity Issued: n/a
★ Average No./Auction: .13
⊙ Average No./Auction: .59

Comments
Spacing between stamps is narrow. Perforations usually touch or cut on one or more sides. Touching or cutting perfs should not be considered a fault. Unused copies are scarce. Original gum should not be expected on unused copies; never hinged examples are extremely rare. Faults are commonplace. Pen canceled copies sell for about half.

Premium Characteristics
Sound condition, reasonably balanced margins (perfs clear of the design are a bonus); neat, clear cancel of the period, if used. Premium unused copies are rare; premium used copies are scarce.

Caveats
Beware ironed-out creases, minor defects, and repairs, including reperfing and regumming. Certificate recommended for unused copies.

5c ORANGE BROWN, Type II
YEAR OF ISSUE: 1861
SCOTT NO. 30

Scarcity
Quantity Issued: scarce
★ Average No./Auction: .79
⊙ Average No./Auction: .23

Comments
Spacing between stamps is narrow at top and bottom, however, side margins are larger than on the preceding 5-cent 1857s. Perfs often touch or cut design. Used copies are scarcer than unused. Original gum should not be expected on unused copies, however, it is more frequently encountered than on other 5-cent 1857s. Never hinged examples are rare. Faults are commonplace. Pen canceled copies sell for about half.

Premium Characteristics
Sound condition, bold color, reasonably balanced margins (perfs clear of the design are a bonus); neat, clear cancel of the period, if used. Premium unused copies are somewhat scarce; premium used copies are very scarce.

Caveats
Beware ironed-out creases, minor defects, and repairs, including reperfing and regumming. Beware fake cancels. Beware copies faked from proofs. Sides must be wide. Certificate essential for used copies and copies on cover, and strongly recommend for unused copies.

Note the margins on the left stamp (Scott No. 29) and three the right stamps (Scott No. 30).

5c BROWN, Type II
YEAR OF ISSUE: 1860
SCOTT NO. 30A

Scarcity
Quantity Issued: n/a
★ Average No./Auction: .21
☉ Average No./Auction: .57

Comments
Spacing between stamps is narrow at top and bottom, however, side margins are larger than on the Scott Nos. 27-29. Perforations usually touch or cut on one or more sides. Touching or cutting perfs should not be considered a fault. Unused copies are scarce; in fact, four to five times scarcer than unused copies of Scott No. 30. Original gum should not be expected on unused copies; never hinged examples are very rare. Faults are commonplace. Pen canceled copies sell for about forty percent.

Premium Characteristics
Sound condition, reasonably balanced margins (within the limits of the issue); neat, clear cancel of the period, if used. Premium copies are scarce.

Caveats
Beware ironed-out creases, minor defects, and repairs, including reperfing and regumming. Sides must be wide. Certificate strongly recommended for unused copies.

10c GREEN, Type I
YEAR OF ISSUE: 1857
SCOTT NO. 31

Scarcity
Quantity Issued: n/a
★ Average No./Auction: .04
☉ Average No./Auction: .31

Comments
Spacing between stamps is wider than other values of this series, nevertheless, perforations typically touch or cut on one or more sides. Touching or cutting perfs are not considered a fault. Irregular perfs are typical. Unused copies are very scarce. Original gum should not be expected on unused copies; never hinged examples are virtually nonexistent. Faults are commonplace. Pen canceled copies sell for about half.

Premium Characteristics
Sound condition, reasonably balanced margins (perfs clear of design, if possible); neat, clear cancel of the period, if used. Design at bottom should be full and strong on premium copies. Premium copies are rare. The illustrated example is nicely centered for this issue. Note irregular perfs.

Caveats
Beware ironed-out creases, minor defects, and repairs, including regumming and reperfing. Beware proofs faked to resemble this stamp. Certificate essential for unused and recommended for used.

10c GREEN, Type II
YEAR OF ISSUE: 1857
SCOTT NO. 32

Scarcity
Quantity Issued: n/a
★ Average No./Auction: .08
☉ Average No./Auction: .70

Comments
Spacing between stamps is wider than other values of this series, nevertheless, perforations typically touch or cut on one or more sides. Touching or cutting perfs are not considered a fault, nor are irregular perfs considered a fault. Unused copies are scarce. Original gum should not be expected on unused copies; never hinged examples are extremely rare. Faults are commonplace. Pen canceled copies sell for about forty percent.

Premium Characteristics
Sound condition, reasonably balanced margins (perfs clear of the design, if possible); neat, clear cancel of the period, if used. Premium copies are very scarce.

Caveats
Beware ironed-out creases, minor defects, and repairs, including regumming and reperfing. Certificate strongly recommended for unused copies.

10c GREEN, Type II
YEAR OF ISSUE: 1857
SCOTT NO. 33

Scarcity
Quantity Issued: n/a
★ Average No./Auction: .11
☉ Average No./Auction: .49

Comments
Spacing between stamps is wider than other values of this series, nevertheless, perforations typically touch or cut on one or more sides. Touching or cutting perfs should not be considered a fault, nor are irregular perfs considered a fault. Unused copies are very scarce.

Original gum should not be expected on unused copies; never hinged examples are extremely rare. Faults are commonplace. Pen canceled copies sell for about forty percent.

Premium Characteristics
Sound condition, reasonably balanced margins (with perfs clear of design, if possible); neat, clear cancel of the period, if used. Premium unused copies are very scarce; premium used copies are scarce.

Caveats
Beware ironed-out creases, minor defects, and repairs, including regumming and reperfing. Certificate recommended for unused copies.

Note the centering and margins on these 10-cent 1857s. Also note the condition of the perforations, which are typical for this issue.

10c GREEN, Type IV
YEAR OF ISSUE: 1857
SCOTT NO. 34

Scarcity
Quantity Issued: n/a
★ Average No./Auction: .02
◉ Average No./Auction: .49

Comments
Spacing between stamps is wider than other values of this series, nevertheless, perforations typically touch or cut on one or more sides. Touching or cutting perfs should not be considered a fault, nor are irregular perfs considered a fault. Unused copies are among the rarest of U.S. stamps and are usually faulty. Original gum should not be expected on unused copies; never hinged examples are virtually nonexistent. Pen canceled copies sell for about forty percent.

Premium Characteristics
Unused copies are extremely rare, therefore, selectivity in the normal sense is not possible. Used copies: sound condition, balanced margins (perfs clear of design, if possible); neat, clear cancel of the period. Premium used copies are very scarce.

Caveats
Beware ironed-out creases, minor defects, and repairs, including regumming and reperfing. Beware fakes fabricated from Scott Nos. 32 or 33. Certificate essential for unused copies and recommended for used copies.

10c GREEN, Type V
YEAR OF ISSUE: 1857
SCOTT NO. 35

Scarcity
Quantity Issued: n/a
★ Average No./Auction: .55
◉ Average No./Auction: .80

Comments
Vertical and horizontal spacing between stamps is much wider than other 10-cent 1857s, however, centering can still be a problem. Irregular perfs are typical and not considered a fault. Original gum should not be expected on unused copies, however, original gum is more frequently encountered on this stamp than on other 10-cent 1857s. Never hinged examples exist, but are scarce. Faults are commonplace. A great variety of interesting and desirable cancels exist on this issue. Pen canceled copies sell for about half.

Premium Characteristics
Sound condition, reasonably balanced margins with perforations clear of design; neat, clear cancel of the period on used stamps. Premium unused copies are scarce; premium used copies, are more readily obtainable than either premium unused copies or other 10-cent 1857s.

Caveats
Beware ironed-out creases, minor defects, and repairs, including regumming and reperfing. Certificate recommended for unused.

Examples of Scott No. 35. Note the wider margins, especially on the sides. Also, note the occasional irregular perfs, which are typical.

12c BLACK
YEAR OF ISSUE: 1857
SCOTT NO. 36

Scarcity
Quantity Issued: n/a
★ Average No./Auction: .14
☉ Average No./Auction: .20

Comments
Spacing between stamps is very narrow. Perfs usually hug the frameline and typically touch or cut on one or more sides. Touching or cutting perfs are not considered a fault. The illustrated example is a gem copy with margins superior to most. Note the irregular nature of the perfs, some taller, some shorter, which is typical. Faults are commonplace on this issue. Original gum should not be expected on unused copies; never hinged examples are very rare. Pen canceled copies sell for about half.

Premium Characteristics
Sound condition, strong color, reasonable centering (within the limits of the issue); neat, clear cancel of the period, if used. Premium copies are scarce (considerably more scarce than No. 36b).

Caveats
Beware ironed-out creases, minor defects, and repairs, including regumming and reperfing. Certificate recommended for unused copies.

12c BLACK
YEAR OF ISSUE: 1859
SCOTT NO. 36b

Scarcity
Quantity Issued: n/a
★ Average No./Auction: .31
☉ Average No./Auction: .14

Comments
Spacing between stamps is slightly wider than on Scott No. 36, nevertheless, perforations typically touch or cut on one or more sides. Touching or cutting perfs are not considered a fault. Original gum should not be expected on unused copies, however, original gum is more frequently encountered than on Scott No. 36. Never hinged examples are scarce. Faults are commonplace. Pen canceled copies sell for about half.

Premium Characteristics
Sound condition, reasonable centering (within the limits of the issue); neat, clear cancel of the period, if used. Premium copies are scarce, but not nearly as scarce as premium copies of Scott No. 36.

Caveats
Beware ironed-out creases, minor defects, and repairs, including regumming and reperfing. Certificate recommended for unused.

Compare the margins on the left stamp (Scott No. 36), with those on the right stamp (Scott No. 36b). The illustrated copy of Scott No. 36b shows how large side margins can be, although actual size will vary from stamp to stamp depending on centering. Scott No. 36 never possesses margins that large.

narrow with virtually no space between stamps horizontally, making balanced margins on four sides virtually impossible. However, copies with attractive centering exist, such as the illustrated example, which is a gem. Perfs often touch or cut at top or bottom and that should not be considered a fault. Several nice shades exist and many attractive cancels. Original gum should not be expected on unused copies; never hinged examples are rare. Faults are commonplace. Pen canceled copies sell for about half.

24c GRAY LILAC
YEAR OF ISSUE: 1860
SCOTT NO. 37

Scarcity
Quantity Issued: n/a
★ Average No./Auction: .63
◉ Average No./Auction: .78

Comments
Spacing between stamps is very

Premium Characteristics
Sound condition, reasonable centering and color; neat, clear cancel of the period, if used. Premium copies are scarce.

Caveats
Beware ironed-out creases, minor defects, and repairs, including regumming and reperfing. Certificate recommended for unused copies.

Comments
Color routinely appears somewhat dingy. Spacing between stamps is extremely narrow. Perforations typically touch or cut on one or more sides. Touching or cutting perfs are not considered a fault. The illustrated example is about as nice as they come. Note the condition of the perfs, which is typical. Original gum should not be expected on unused copies; never hinged examples are rare. Faults are commonplace. Pen canceled copies sell for about half.

30c ORANGE
YEAR OF ISSUE: 1860
SCOTT NO. 38

Scarcity
Quantity Issued: n/a
★ Average No./Auction: .82
◉ Average No./Auction: .62

Premium Characteristics
Sound condition, reasonable margins (within the limits of the issue), good color (within the limits of the issue); neat, clear cancel of the period, if used. Premium copies are very scarce.

Caveats
Beware ironed-out creases, minor defects, and repairs, including regumming and reperfing. Certificate recommended for unused.

90c BLUE
YEAR OF ISSUE: 1857
SCOTT NO. 39

Scarcity
Quantity Issued: 25,000 est.
★ Average No./Auction: 1.00
⊙ Average No./Auction: .25

Comments
Spacing between stamps is narrow but not as narrow as the 30-cent. Margins are usually tightest at top or bottom. Touching or cutting perfs, especially at top or bottom, should

not be considered a fault. Original gum should not be expected on unused copies, however, original gum is more frequently encountered than on either the 24-cent or 30-cent. Never hinged examples are rare. Faults are commonplace, especially on used copies. Clear, discernable cancels are necessary to determine genuineness. Pen canceled copies sell for a considerable discount.

Premium Characteristics
Sound condition, reasonable centering, solid color; neat, clear of the period, if used. Premiums unused copies are scarce; genuinely used premium copies (well centered, fault free) are exceedingly rare.

Caveats
This issue is especially prone to reperfing and repairing, especially used copies. Beware ironed-out creases, minor defects, and repairs, including regumming and reperfing. This stamp catalogues substantially more used than unused, therefore, beware fake cancels. Certificate recommended for unused copies and is essential for used copies.

High values of the 1857 series. Note margins and typical appearance of the perforations.

1857-60 SERIES
REPRINTS OF 1875
SCOTT NOS. 40-47

Scarcity
Quantity Issued:
No. 40	(1c)	3,846
No. 41	(3c)	479
No. 42	(5c)	878
No. 43	(10c)	516
No. 44	(12c)	489
No. 45	(24c)	479
No. 46	(30c)	480
No. 47	(90c)	454

★ Average No./Auction:
No. 40	.58
No. 41	.20
No. 42	.34
No. 43	.31
No. 44	.19
No. 45	.16
No. 46	.23
No. 47	.25

Comments
Issued on white paper without gum. Not valid for postage. The reprints are perforated 12 rather than 15 as were the originals. Colors are generally brighter than the regularly issued stamps. Perforations typically touch or cut on one or more sides; appealing centering is virtually impossible to find. Touching or cutting perfs are not considered a fault. Irregular perfs, often ragged looking, are common on this series and not considered a fault. Scissor separated perfs are also common to this issue and not considered a fault. A greater percentage of the reprints are sound, as compared to the regularly issued stamps. Approximately 70-90 percent of those surveyed were sound.

Premium Characteristics
Sound condition, reasonable appearance (the enlarged examples above illustrate the perforation and margin shortcomings of the issue), and good color. Premium copies are rare and difficult. The illustrated examples are about as nice as one can expect to find.

Caveats
Beware ironed-out creases, minor defects, and repairs, including reperfing. Beware fakes created from proofs. Certificate essential.

1861 SERIES, AUGUST ISSUE
SCOTT NOS. 55-62

Scarcity
Quantity Issued: 12-15 each est. (except Nos. 58 and 60 which are more abundant, and No. 56 which is much more abundant).

★ Average No./Auction:

No. 55	.02
No. 56	.55
No. 57	.01
No. 58	.15
No. 59	.02
No. 60	.07
No. 61	.01
No. 62	.01

Note: Some controversy exists over whether this issue are stamps, essays or proofs. The author takes no position in this matter. They are listed here in their traditional order and under their traditional numbers merely for the sake of convenience.

Comments
Stamps are more heavily inked than the subsequent issue, colors brighter and more vivid. Bold impressions are usual for this issue. Perforations typically touch or cut on one or more sides and that should not be considered a fault. Short or irregular perforations are typical. Original gum has generally been preserved on all values except the 10-cent and 24-cent. Original gum for this issue is naturally brownish, not toned. Never hinged examples, if they exist, are of the greatest rarity, except for Scott No. 56, which are occasionally found. Faults are commonplace and to be expected.

Premium Characteristics
Ideally, fault free, balanced margins to the extent possible, and good color; however, the rarity of this issue doesn't permit the selectivity normally possible.

Caveats
Beware dangerous fakes of the 12-cent value. Also, fakes from proofs on the 1-cent, 5-cent, 30-cent and 90-cent values. The majority of the rarer values are faulty. Certificate essential.

10c DARK GREEN
YEAR OF ISSUE: 1861
SCOTT NO. 62B

Scarcity
Quantity Issued: n/a
★ Average No./Auction: .00
☉ Average No./Auction: .42

Note: No unused copies were encountered in the survey.

Comments
Typically small margined and poorly centered. Touching or cutting perfs should not be considered a fault, however, copies with perfs clear of design exist. Irregular perfs are usual for this issue. Faults are commonplace. Unused copies are extremely rare. Original gum should not be expected on unused copies; never hinged examples are virtually nonexistent.

Premium Characteristics
Sound condition, reasonable centering (within the limits of the issue), good color; neat, clear cancel for period on used copies. Premium copies are extremely difficult. The rarity of unused copies does not permit selectivity in the normal sense.

Caveats
Beware the usual faults, including repairs. Certificate essential for unused and recommended for used.

1c BLUE
YEAR OF ISSUE: 1861
SCOTT NO. 63

Scarcity
Quantity Issued: n/a
★ Average No./Auction: .46

Comments
Comes in a variety of shades from pale blue to very dark blue and ultramarine. Dark blue and ultramarine command a premium. The indigo shade is a rarity (there is controversy over whether it exists). The shades are difficult to distinguish without experience. This stamp is typically tightly margined and difficult to find well centered. Irregular perfs are commonplace and not considered a fault. The illustrated example shows typical perfs. Full original gum should not be expected on unused copies; never hinged copies exist, and although not rare, command a premium. Faults are commonplace.

Premium Characteristics
Sound condition, balanced margins, good color; full original gum (either very lightly hinged or never hinged) if unused; neat, clear cancel of the period, if used. Premium copies are difficult.

Caveats
Beware the usual minor faults and repairs, including regumming and reperfing. Certificate recommended for unused.

3c PINK
YEAR OF ISSUE: 1861
SCOTT NO. 64

Scarcity
Quantity Issued: scarce
★ Average No./Auction: .16
⊚ Average No./Auction: .34

Comments
The pink shade is very difficult to identify without experience. Touching or cutting perfs are typical as the illustration demonstrates (bottom of page 27). Irregular perfs are commonplace and not considered a fault. Nicely centered copies are difficult. Original gum should not be expected on unused copies; never hinged examples are exceedingly rare. Original gum is typically brownish. This stamp usually contains faults.

A pigeon blood pink shade exists (Scott No. 64a), which is very rare and much more valuable. It is extremely difficult to locate in any condition. In fact, no copies (either unused or used) were encountered in the auction survey.

Premium Characteristics
Sound condition, reasonable centering, solid color; neat, clear cancel of the period, if used. Premium unused copies are exceedingly rare; premium used copies are very difficult.

Caveats
Beware ironed-out creases, minor faults, and repairs, including regumming and reperfing. Certificate absolutely essential.

3c ROSE
YEAR OF ISSUE: 1861
SCOTT NO. 65

Scarcity
Quantity Issued: n/a
★ Average No./Auction: .53

Comments
Exists in a countless variety of shades, some of which of are often confused with the more valuable pinks of Scott No. 64. Full original gum should not be expected on unused copies; never hinged copies exist, and although not rare, command a premium. This stamp is typically tightly margined and difficult to find well centered. Many copies are faulty but because of the large population, sound copies are not difficult to find. Many interesting cancels, including fancy cancels, exist, some very rare and worth a substantial premium. Stamp is worth a considerable premium on patriotic cover.

Premium Characteristics
Sound condition, balanced margins, good color, full original gum (either very lightly hinged or never hinged) if unused; neat, clear cancel of the period, if used. Premium copies are not common, but available.

Caveats
Beware the usual minor faults and repairs, including regumming and reperfing. Certificate recommended for never hinged original gum and those with expensive cancels.

3c LAKE
YEAR OF ISSUE: 1861
SCOTT NO. 66

Scarcity
Quantity Issued: scarce
★ Average No./Auction: .24
⊚ Average No./Auction: n/a

Comments
Considered by many to be a proof, this stamp is exceedingly rare used. Touching or cutting perfs are typical and not considered a fault. Original gum is more frequently encountered on this stamp; some experts estimate that as many as 75 percent still retain original gum. Never hinged examples exist but are rare. Nicely centered copies are difficult. Unlike most nineteenth century stamps, this one is typically encountered in sound condition. Only about 25 percent of the copies surveyed were faulty. It is difficult to locate nicely centered.

Premium Characteristics
Sound condition, reasonable centering and margins, solid color. Premium copies are very scarce, centering being the most difficult element.

Caveats
Beware faults and repairs, including regumming (although it is not as frequently encountered as on other issues) and reperfing. Certificate strongly recommended for unused, and essential for used.

Examples of 3-cent 1861s. Note margins and typical irregularities in the perforations.

5c BUFF
YEAR OF ISSUE: 1861
SCOTT NO. 67

Scarcity
Quantity Issued: 600,000 est.
★ Average No./Auction: .13
⊚ Average No./Auction: .77

Comments
This stamp is very rare unused. Typically, it has a drab, indistinct appearance and is usually tightly margined. Copies with balanced margins clear of the design are very scarce and worth a substantial premium. Most copies are faulty or repaired due to the sub-standard grade of paper used for printing. Full original gum should not be expected on unused copies; never hinged copies, if they exist, are exceedingly rare. The stamp is worth a substantial premium on patriotic cover. Also exists with a variety of fancy cancels, some of which are worth a substantial premium.

Premium Characteristics
Sound condition, balanced margins, sharp impression, crisp color; neat, clear cancel of the period, if used. Premium unused copies are extremely rare; premium used copies are very scarce.

Caveats
This stamp is usually faulty. Beware repairs, including regumming and reperfing. Certificate essential for unused copy and recommended for used copy.

10c YELLOW GREEN
YEAR OF ISSUE: 1861
SCOTT NO. 68

Scarcity
Quantity Issued: 25,000,000 est.
★ Average No./Auction: .34
⊚ Average No./Auction: .54

Comments
This stamp is somewhat tightly margined, although not as tightly as Scott No. 67. Copies with large, balanced margins clear of the design are very scarce and worth a substantial premium. The illustrated example is nicely margined for this issue. Note the typically irregular perfs, which are not considered a fault. Full original gum should not be expected on unused copies; never hinged copies are very scarce. Faults are commonplace. The stamp is worth a substantial premium on patriotic cover.

Premium Characteristics
Sound condition, balanced margins, good color, and full original gum; neat, clear cancel of the period, if used. Premium unused copies are inexplicably difficult and command substantial premiums; premium used copies are moderately difficult.

Caveats
Beware faults and repairs, including regumming and reperfing. Certificate strongly recommended for unused.

12c BLACK
YEAR OF ISSUE: 1861
SCOTT NO. 69

Scarcity
Quantity Issued: 3,500,000 est.
★ Average No./Auction: .40
⊘ Average No./Auction: .61

Comments
This stamp tends to be small margined. The illustrated example is as nicely centered as one could want. Copies with large balanced margins are scarce and worth a substantial premium. Many copies are faulty or repaired. Full original gum should not be expected on unused copies; NH copies are scarce. Faults are commonplace. Stamp is worth a substantial premium on patriotic cover.

Premium Characteristics
Sound condition, balanced margins, good color; neat, clear cancel of period, if used. Premium unused copies are rare; premium used copies are scarce.

Caveats
Beware faults and repairs, including regumming and reperfing. Beware cleaned copies passing for unused. Certificate for unused copy strongly recommended.

24c RED LILAC
YEAR OF ISSUE: 1861
SCOTT NO. 70

Scarcity
Quantity Issued: 40,000 est.
★ Average No./Auction: .07
⊘ Average No./Auction: .37

Comments
This stamp exists in a multitude of shades which are almost impossible to distinguish without expertise. The prominent shades are collectible. Some shades are rather dingy in appearance, but that should not be counted against them. This stamp is tightly margined and usually touches or cuts on at least one side; refer to the illustration on page 31. Irregular perfs are commonplace and not considered a fault. Full original gum should not be expected on unused copies; never hinged copies are exceedingly rare. Faults are endemic. The stamp is worth a substantial premium on patriotic cover.

Premium Characteristics
Sound condition, balanced margins and distinct color, within the limitations of the issue; neat, clear cancel of the period, if used. Premium copies are extremely difficult.

Caveats
Beware faults and repairs, including regumming and reperfing. Beware color changelings passing as steel blue shade. Certificate strongly recommended for unused copies, and essential for both unused and used copies of Scott Nos. 70a, 70c, and 70d.

30c ORANGE
YEAR OF ISSUE: 1861
SCOTT NO. 71

Scarcity
Quantity Issued: 3,300,000 est.
★ Average No./Auction: .31
⊚ Average No./Auction: .59

Comments
This stamp typically has an indistinct, washed-out appearance. Even copies acknowledged to be superb lack contrast and the usual eye appeal associated with other stamps. It is tightly margined; the illustrated example is very nicely centered for this issue. Copies with balanced margins clear of the design are difficult and worth a substantial premium. Faults are endemic. The illustration on page 31 shows typical margins. Irregular perfs are commonplace and not considered a fault. Full original gum should not be expected on unused copies; never hinged copies, if they exist, are exceedingly rare. Stamp is worth a substantial premium on patriotic cover. Certain cancels also command a premium.

Premium Characteristics
Sound condition, balanced margins, good color (within the limits of the issue); neat, clear cancel of the period, if used. Premium copies are very difficult.

Caveats
Beware faults and repairs, including regumming and reperfing. Certificate recommended for unused and for used copies on patriotic cover.

90c BLUE
YEAR OF ISSUE: 1861
SCOTT NO. 72

Scarcity
Quantity Issued: 400,000 est.
★ Average No./Auction: .43
⊚ Average No./Auction: .68

Comments
This stamp is not as tightly margined as others of the series, and margins are typically larger at top and bottom than at the sides due to spacing of the subjects. Refer to the illustration on page 31. Three major shades exist: blue, pale blue and dark blue, with dark blue worth slightly more. Irregular perfs are commonplace and not considered a fault. Full original gum should not be expected on unused copies; never hinged copies, are known, but are very scarce. Faults are commonplace.

Premium Characteristics
Sound condition, balanced margins, good color; neat, clear cancel of the period, if used. Premium copies are difficult. The illustrated example is a gem of uncommon quality.

Caveats
Beware faults and repairs, including regumming and reperfing. Beware cleaned copies passing as unused. Beware faked green cancels. Certificate strongly recommended for unused, and essential for stamp on cover.

Examples of the 1861 issue illustrating centering, margins, and typical perforations.

2c BLACK
YEAR OF ISSUE: 1863
SCOTT NO. 73

Scarcity
Quantity Issued: 250,000,000 est.
★ Average No./Auction: .65

Comments
This stamp is tightly margined.

Unused copies with balanced margins clear of the design are very scarce and worth a substantial premium. Faults are commonplace. Used copies are abundant (and were not surveyed), so an adequate population of sound examples exists. Full original gum should not be expected on unused copies; never hinged copies exist, but are very scarce. Stamp is worth an enormous premium on patriotic cover. Many desirable cancels exist, some worth substantial premiums.

Premium Characteristics
Sound condition, balanced margins, intact original gum; neat, clear cancel of the period, if used. Premium unused copies are very scarce; premium used copies are not scarce, but nevertheless command premiums.

Caveats
Beware faults and repairs, including regumming and reperfing. Certificate recommended for unused copies and essential for copies on patriotic cover.

3c SCARLET
YEAR OF ISSUE: 1861
SCOTT NO. 74

Scarcity
Quantity Issued: 100 est.
★ Average No./Auction: .12
⊘ Average No./Auction: n/a

Comments
Considered by many to be a proof or essay. Used copies typically contain four horizontal black pen strokes, which are devaluation marks made on presentation or sample copies (copies

exist with and without original gum). The color of the pen-stroke cancelled copies is much stronger and clearer (perhaps they are from a separate printing). This stamp is very rare genuinely postally used. It is tightly margined and perfs often touch or cut the design on at least one side. Irregular perfs are commonplace and not considered a fault. This stamp is usually faulty or repaired. Copies with full original gum are somewhat scarce; never hinged copies are rare.

Premium Characteristics
Sound condition, balanced margins, good color, and full original gum. Premium copies are exceedingly rare.

Caveats
Beware fakes made from proofs. Beware faults and repairs, including regumming. Certificate strongly recommended for unused copies and essential for postally used copies.

5c RED BROWN
YEAR OF ISSUE: 1862
SCOTT NO. 75

Scarcity
Quantity Issued: 1,000,000 est.
★ Average No./Auction: .39
⊘ Average No./Auction: .58

Comments
This stamp is tightly margined; the

illustrated example is typical. Perforations usually touch or cut design. Copies with balanced margins clear of the design are scarce and worth a premium. Irregular perfs are frequently encountered and not considered a fault. Faults are commonplace. Two major shades exist: red brown and dark red brown. Full original gum should not be expected on unused copies; never hinged copies exist, but are very rare. Stamp is worth a substantial premium on patriotic cover.

Premium Characteristics
Sound condition, balanced margins, intact original gum; neat, clear cancel of period, if used. Premium unused copies are rare; premium used copies are scarce.

Caveats
Beware faults and repairs, including regumming and reperfing. Certificate recommended for unused copies and for copies on patriotic cover.

5c BROWN
YEAR OF ISSUE: 1861
SCOTT NO. 76

Scarcity
Quantity Issued: 6,500,000 est.
★ Average No./Auction: .22

Comments
This stamp is small margined and perforations almost always touch or cut the design on at least one side (the illustrated example is beautifully centered for this issue). Copies with balanced margins clear of the design are scarce and worth a premium. Irregular perfs are frequently encountered and not considered a fault. Impressions are typically more crisp than previous two varieties. A black-brown shade exists and is very desirable. Faults are commonplace. Full original gum should not be expected on unused copies; never hinged copies exist, but are very rare. Stamp is worth a substantial premium on patriotic cover.

Premium Characteristics
Sound condition, balanced margins, intact original gum, neat, clear cancel of the period, if used. Premium unused copies are rare; premium used copies are scarce.

Caveats
Beware faults and repairs, including regumming and reperfing. Certificate recommended for unused copies and for copies on patriotic cover.

15c BLACK
YEAR OF ISSUE: 1866
SCOTT NO. 77

Scarcity
Quantity Issued: 2,139,000 est.
★ Average No./Auction: .22

Comments
This stamp is small margined. Perforations typically touch or cut design. Copies with balanced margins clear of the design are scarce and worth a premium. Irregular perfs are frequently encountered and not considered a fault (note the perfs in the illustration). Full original gum should not be expected on unused copies; never hinged copies exist, but are very rare. Faults are commonplace.

Premium Characteristics
Sound condition, balanced margins, intact original gum; neat, clear cancel of the period, if used. Premium unused copies are rare; premium used copies are scarce.

Caveats
Beware faults and repairs, including regumming and reperfing. Certificate recommended for unused copies.

24c LILAC
YEAR OF ISSUE: 1863
SCOTT NO. 78

Scarcity
Quantity Issued: 9,620,000 est.
★ Average No./Auction: .09 *

* Note: Refer to the introduction regarding frequency anomalies.

Comments
This stamp exists in a multitude of shades that are almost impossible to distinguish without expertise. The blackish violet shade is the rarest and commands an enormous premium. This issue is, by its nature, dingy in appearance, so that should not be counted against it. It is tightly margined and usually touches or cuts on at least one side. The illustrated example is a gem with uncommonly large margins. Irregular perfs are frequently encountered and not considered a fault. Full original gum should not be expected on unused copies; never hinged copies, if they exist, are rare. Faults are commonplace.

Premium Characteristics
Sound condition, balanced margins clear of design if possible, intact original gum; neat, clear cancel of the period, if used. Premium used copies are scarce; premium unused copies are rare.

Caveats
Beware faults and repairs, including regumming and reperfing. Certificate recommended for unused copies.

Examples of Scott No. 78. Note margins, centering, and perforations.

GRILLED ISSUES OF 1867 GENERAL COMMENTS

Typically, two or more grill varieties exist for each denomination. Since the general characteristics of each denomination remain more or less the same, regardless of the grill type, they are listed here by denomination. Characteristics unique to a specific stamp are given under an individual stamp's listing. Illustrations, too, have been grouped and appear with the general descriptions. The illustrated stamps are neither the best nor the worst examples of a given issue, but are representative of what can be expected with regard to general quality, centering, perforations, and cancels.

1c DENOMINATIONS (Scott Nos. 85A, 86 and 92)
Typically small margined; perforations usually touch or cut design on at least one side. Typically faulty. Irregular perfs are commonplace and not considered a fault. Full original gum should not be expected on unused copies.

2c DENOMINATIONS (Scott Nos. 84, 85B, 87 and 93)
Typically tightly margined; perforations usually touch or cut design on at least one side. Typically faulty. Irregular perfs are commonplace and not considered a fault. Full original gum should not be expected on unused copies.

3c DENOMINATIONS (Scott Nos. 79, 82, 83, 85, 85C, 88 and 94)
Typically tightly margined; perforations usually touch or cut design on at least one side. Typically faulty. Irregular perfs are commonplace and not considered a fault. Full original gum should not be expected on unused copies.

5c DENOMINATIONS (Scott Nos. 80 and 95)

Typically tightly margined; perforations usually touch or cut design on at least one side. Typically faulty. Irregular perfs are commonplace and not considered a fault. Full original gum should not be expected on unused copies.

10c DENOMINATIONS (85D, 89 and 96)

This stamp is small margined although margins are somewhat larger than on other values of the series. Perforations typically touch or cut the design on one or more sides. Typically faulty. Irregular perfs are commonplace and not considered a fault. Full original gum should not be expected on unused copies.

12c DENOMINATIONS (85E, 90 and 97)

This stamp is small margined, but margins are not as tight as on the 2-cent or 5-cent values. Nevertheless, perfs often touch or cut on at least one side of the design. Typically faulty. The illustrated examples are nicer than usual. Irregular perfs are commonplace and not considered a fault. Full original gum should not be expected on unused copies.

15c DENOMINATIONS (85F, 91 and 98)

This stamp is small margined. Perfs usually touch or cut the design on one or more sides. Most copies are faulty. Irregular perfs are frequently encountered and not considered a fault. Full original gum should not be expected on unused copies.

3c ROSE, A Grill
YEAR OF ISSUE: 1867
SCOTT NO. 79

Scarcity
Quantity Issued: 50,000 est.
★ Average No./Auction: .05
⊙ Average No./Auction: .22

Comments
Never hinged copies, if they exist, are rare. Irregular perfs are standard.

Premium Characteristics
Sound condition, reasonably balanced margins (clear of design if possible), intact original gum; neat, clear cancel of the period, if used. Both premium unused and used copies are very rare.

Caveats
Beware faults and repairs, including regumming and reperfing. Beware fake grills (essay grills also exist). Certificate essential.

OTHER A GRILL ISSUES
SCOTT NO. 80, 5c BROWN
SCOTT NO. 81, 30c ORANGE

Scarcity
Quantity Issued:
No. 80   2,000 est.
No. 81   2,000 est.

Comments
Only about 4-6 copies of each stamp are known. These stamps suffers from the same problems typical of their ungrilled counterparts: narrow margins, perforations touching or cutting on one or more sides, irregular perfs, faults, heavy cancellations. The faults are irrelevant, as is the issue of original gum and hinging. The population is simply too restricted to permit selectivity in the normal sense.

Premium Characteristics
Premium copies, if they exist (which is doubtful) would be of the utmost rarity.

Caveats
Beware fakes. Certificate absolutely essential.

3c ROSE, B Grill
YEAR OF ISSUE: 1867
SCOTT NO. 82

Scarcity
Quantity Issued: n/a

Comments
This stamp is exceedingly rare and only known used. Lester Brookman reported that only four copies were known, all on a single cover. These copies have since been removed from the cover.

Caveats
Suspect any copies not fully documented. Certificate absolutely essential.

3c ROSE, C Grill
YEAR OF ISSUE: 1867
SCOTT NO. 83

Scarcity
Quantity Issued: 300,000 est.
★ Average No./Auction: .18
⊙ Average No./Auction: .41

Comments
Used copies are usually heavily canceled. Never hinged copies, if they exist, are of the utmost rarity.

Premium Characteristics
Sound condition, reasonably balanced margins (clear of design, if possible), intact original gum; neat, clear cancel of the period, if used. Premium unused copies are rare; premium used copies are very scarce.

Caveats
Beware faults and repairs, including regumming and reperfing. Fake grills are seldom encountered on this issue. Certificate essential.

2c BLACK, D Grill
YEAR OF ISSUE: 1867
SCOTT NO. 84

Scarcity
Quantity Issued: 200,000 est.
★ Average No./Auction: .08
⊘ Average No./Auction: .26

Comments
Used copies are usually heavily canceled.
Never hinged copies, if they exist, are
very rare. Fake grills exist.

Premium Characteristics
Sound condition, reasonably balanced
margins, intact original gum; neat, clear
cancel of the period, if used. Premium
unused copies are rare; premium unused
copies are scarce.

Caveats
Beware faults and repairs, including
regumming and reperfing. Beware fake
grills. Certificate essential.

3c ROSE, D Grill
YEAR OF ISSUE: 1867
SCOTT NO. 85

Scarcity
Quantity Issued: 500,000 est.
★ Average No./Auction: .06
⊘ Average No./Auction: .59

Comments
Never hinged copies, if they exist, are
very rare. Fake grills exist.

Premium Characteristics
Sound condition, reasonably balanced
margins (clear of the design, if possible),
good color, and original gum; neat, clear
cancel of the period, if used. Premium
copies are very scarce.

Caveats
Beware faults and repairs, including
regumming and reperfing. Beware fake
grills. Certificate essential.

1c BLUE, Z Grill
YEAR OF ISSUE: 1867
SCOTT NO. 85A

Scarcity
Quantity Issued: 2 copies known

Comments
Both known copies are used. Because of
rarity, each stamp stands on its own
merits.

Caveats
Certificate essential.

2c BLACK, Z Grill
YEAR OF ISSUE: 1867
SCOTT NO. 85B

Scarcity
Quantity Issued: 500,000 est.
★ Average No./Auction: .11
⊘ Average No./Auction: .39

Comments
Never hinged copies, if they exist, are
exceedingly rare. Genuine grills are
usually sharp and clear. Fake grills exist.

Premium Characteristics
Sound condition, reasonably balanced
margins, original gum; neat, clear light
cancel of the period, if used. Premium
copies are extremely difficult.

Caveats
Beware faults and repairs, including
regumming and reperfing. Beware fake
grills. Certificate essential.

3c ROSE, Z Grill
YEAR OF ISSUE: 1867
SCOTT NO. 85C

Scarcity
Quantity Issued: 500,000 est.
★ Average No./Auction: .06
⊘ Average No./Auction: .13

Comments
Never hinged copies, if they exist, are rare. Fake grills exist.

Premium Characteristics
Sound condition, reasonably balanced margins (clear of the design, if possible) intact original gum; neat, clear cancel of the period, if used. Premium copies are very rare.

Caveats
Beware faults and repairs, including regumming and reperfing. Beware fake grills. Certificate essential.

10c GREEN, Z Grill
DATE OF ISSUE: 1867
SCOTT NO. 85D

Scarcity
Quantity Issued: 2,000 est.

Comments
This stamp is exceedingly rare. Only about five copies are known, all used. It suffers from the same problems typical of stamps of the era: narrow margins,

perforations touching or cutting on one or more sides, faults, heavy cancellations. The faults are irrelevant, however, as is the issue of original gum and hinging. The population of this rarity is simply too restricted to permit selectivity in the normal sense.

Caveats
Beware fakes. Certificate absolutely essential.

12c BLACK, Z Grill
YEAR OF ISSUE: 1867
SCOTT NO. 85E

Scarcity
Quantity Issued: 100,000 est.
★ Average No./Auction: .05
⊘ Average No./Auction: .25

Comments
This stamp typically exhibits an intense black color. The majority are faulty. Never hinged copies, if they exist, are exceedingly rare.

Premium Characteristics
Sound condition, large balanced margins, good color; neat, clear cancel of the period, if used. Most copies are either poorly centered or faulty. Premium unused copies are rare; premium used copies are very scarce.

Caveats
Beware faults and repairs, including regumming and reperfing. Beware fake grills. Certificate essential.

15c BLACK, Z Grill
YEAR OF ISSUE: 1867
SCOTT NO. 85F

Scarcity
Quantity Issued: n/a

Comments
A great rarity. Because of rarity, each stamp stands on its own merits.

Caveats
Beware fakes. Certificate essential.

1c BLUE, E Grill
YEAR OF ISSUE: 1867
SCOTT NO. 86

Scarcity
Quantity Issued: 3,000,000 est.
★ Average No./Auction: .15
☉ Average No./Auction: .35

Comments
Grills range from faintly to clearly impressed. Used copies are often heavily canceled. Never hinged copies, if they exist, are rare. Fake grills exist.

Premium Characteristics
Sound condition, good color, balanced margins clear of the design, intact original gum; neat, clear cancel of the period, if used. Premium unused copies are rare; premium used copies are scarce.

Caveats
Beware faults and repairs, including regumming and reperfing. Beware fake grills. Certificate essential.

2c BLACK, E Grill
YEAR OF ISSUE: 1867
SCOTT NO. 87

Scarcity
Quantity Issued: 25,000,000 est.
★ Average No./Auction: .13

Comments
Grills range from faintly to clearly impressed. Never hinged copies exist, but are rare. Fake grills exist.

Premium Characteristics
Sound condition, balanced margins, original gum, and neat, clear cancel of the period, if used. Premium unused copies are rare; premium unused copies are scarce.

Caveats
Beware faults and repairs, including regumming and reperfing. Beware fake grills. Certificate essential on unused.

3c ROSE, E Grill
YEAR OF ISSUE: 1867
SCOTT NO. 88

Scarcity
Quantity Issued: 80,000,000 est.
★ Average No./Auction: .53

Comments
The population of used copies is relatively large, therefore, sound used copies are not as difficult as on previous 3-cent grills. Never hinged copies are rare. Fake grills exist.

Premium Characteristics
Sound condition, balanced margins, good color, original gum if unused; neat, clear cancel of the period, if used. Premium unused copies are very scarce; premium used copies are not common, however, they are more easily located than other 3-cent grills.

Caveats
Beware the usual minor faults and repairs, including regumming and reperfing. Beware fake grills, which although not frequently encountered, do exist. Certificate recommended for unused copies.

General descriptions and illustrations of grilled issues appear on pages 35 and 36.

10c GREEN, E GRILL
YEAR OF ISSUE: 1867
SCOTT NO. 89

Scarcity
Quantity Issued: 1,500,000 est.
★ Average No./Auction: .14
⊙ Average No./Auction: .42

Comments
Never hinged copies, if they exist, are rare. Fake grills exist.

Premium Characteristics
Sound condition, balanced margins, good color, original gum if unused; neat, clear cancel of the period, if used. Premium copies are difficult.

Caveats
Beware faults and repairs, including regumming and reperfing. Beware fake grills. Certificate essential.

12c BLACK, E Grill
YEAR OF ISSUE: 1867
SCOTT NO. 90

Scarcity
Quantity Issued: 1,000,000 est.
★ Average No./Auction: .14
⊙ Average No./Auction: .53

Comments
Never hinged copies are rare. Fake grills exist.

Premium Characteristics
Sound condition, balanced margins, good color, original gum if unused; neat, clear cancel of the period, if used. Premium copies are very scarce.

Caveats
Beware the usual minor faults and repairs, including regumming and reperfing. Beware fake grills. Certificate essential.

15c BLACK, E GRILL
YEAR OF ISSUE: 1867
SCOTT NO. 91

Scarcity
Quantity Issued: 500,000 est.
★ Average No./Auction: .13
⊙ Average No./Auction: .53

Comments
Never hinged copies are rare. Fake grills exist.

Premium Characteristics
Sound condition, balanced margins, good color, original gum if unused; neat, clear cancel of the period, if used. Premium copies are difficult.

Caveats
Beware faults and repairs, including regumming and reperfing. Beware fake grills. Certificate essential.

General descriptions and illustrations of grilled issues appear on pages 35 and 36.

1c BLUE, F Grill
YEAR OF ISSUE: 1867
SCOTT NO. 92

Scarcity
Quantity Issued: 7,000,000 est.
★ Average No./Auction: .09
๏ Average No./Auction: .23

Comments
Never hinged copies are rare. Fake grills exist.

Premium Characteristics
Sound condition, balanced margins, good color, original gum if unused; neat, clear cancel of the period for used. Premium copies are very scarce.

Caveats
Beware the usual minor faults and repairs, including regumming and reperfing. Beware fake grills. Certificate strongly recommended.

2c BLACK, F GRILL
YEAR OF ISSUE: 1867
SCOTT NO. 93

Scarcity
Quantity Issued: 50,000,000 est.
★ Average No./Auction: .24

Comments
Because of its large populations, this is the easiest "Black Jack" to locate with decent centering. Never hinged copies are scarce, but available. Fake grills exist.

Premium Characteristics
Sound condition, balanced margins, good color, original gum if unused; neat, clear cancel of the period, if used. Premium copies are difficult.

Caveats
Beware faults and repairs, including regumming and reperfing. Beware fake grills. Certificate strongly recommended for unused; essential for never hinged.

3c RED, F Grill
YEAR OF ISSUE: 1867
SCOTT NO. 94

Scarcity
Quantity Issued: 225,000,000 est.
★ Average No./Auction: .18

Comments
The population of used copies is relatively large, therefore, sound used copies are not as difficult as other 3-cent grills. Many desirable cancels are found on this issue, some of which are worth many times the base price of the stamp. Never hinged copies are scarce, but available. Used stamps, especially, tend to have a dull, washed-out appearance. Fake grills are rarely encountered.

Premium Characteristics
Sound condition, balanced margins, good color, original gum if unused; neat, clear cancel of the period, if used. Premium unused copies are very scarce. Premium used copies are not scarce.

Caveats
Beware the usual minor faults and repairs, including regumming and reperfing. Certificate recommended for unused.

5c BROWN, F GRILL
YEAR OF ISSUE: 1867
SCOTT NO. 95

Scarcity
Quantity Issued: 680,000 est.
★ Average No./Auction: .23
⊙ Average No./Auction: .24

Comments
Never hinged copies are rare. Fake grills exist.

Premium Characteristics
Sound condition, reasonably balanced margins, good color, original gum, if unused; neat, clear cancel of the period, if used. Premium copies are very difficult.

Caveats
Beware faults and repairs, including regumming and reperfing. Beware fake grills. Certificate essential.

10c YELLOW GREEN, F Grill
YEAR OF ISSUE: 1867
SCOTT NO. 96

Scarcity
Quantity Issued: 3,800,000 est.
★ Average No./Auction: .24
⊙ Average No./Auction: .45

Comments
Never hinged copies are rare. Fake grills exist.

Premium Characteristics
Sound condition, balanced margins, good color, original gum, if unused; neat, clear postmark of the period, if used. Premium copies, especially unused, are very scarce.

Caveats
Beware the usual minor faults and repairs, including regumming and reperfing. Beware fake grills. Certificate recommended for unused.

12c BLACK, F GRILL
YEAR OF ISSUE: 1867
SCOTT NO. 97

Scarcity
Quantity Issued: 2,600,000 est.
★ Average No./Auction: .13
⊙ Average No./Auction: .48

Comments
The 12-cent "F" grills commonly have excess black ink in the margins due to bad plate burnishing. Never hinged

copies are very rare. Fake grills exist.

Premium Characteristics
Sound condition, balanced margins, good color, original gum if unused; neat, clear cancel of the period for used. Premium copies are very difficult.

Caveats
Beware faults and repairs, including regumming and reperfing. Beware fake grills. Certificate recommended.

General descriptions and illustrations of grilled issues appear on pages 35 and 36.

15c BLACK, F Grill
YEAR OF ISSUE: 1867
SCOTT NO. 98

Scarcity
Quantity Issued: 2,000,000 est.
★ Average No./Auction: .13
⊙ Average No./Auction: .46

Comments
Never hinged copies are very rare. Fake grills exist.

Premium Characteristics
Sound condition, balanced margins, good color, original gum, if unused; neat, clear cancel of the period, if used. Premium copies are very scarce.

Caveats
Beware faults and repairs, including regumming and reperfing. Beware fake grills. Certificate recommended, especially for unused.

are very tough. Most copies are faulty. Irregular perfs are frequently encountered and not considered a fault. Color is notoriously poor. Full original gum should not be expected on unused copies; never hinged copies are very rare. The illustrated examples give an idea of typical quality. Fake grills exist.

24c LILAC, F Grill
YEAR OF ISSUE: 1867
SCOTT NO. 99

Scarcity
Quantity Issued: 200,000 est.
★ Average No./Auction: .15
⊙ Average No./Auction: .28

Comments
This stamp is tightly margined. Perfs almost always touch or cut the design on one or more sides. It appears less frequently at auction than either the 30-cent or 90-cent F-grills, and nice copies

Premium Characteristics
Sound condition, reasonably balanced margins (within the limits of the issue), good color (to the extent possible), original gum, if unused; neat, clear cancel of the period, if used. Premium copies are exceedingly rare. This is one issue that cannot be held to an unrealistically high standard of quality.

Caveats
Beware faults and repairs, including regumming and reperfing. Beware fake grills. Certificate essential.

30c ORANGE, F GRILL
YEAR OF ISSUE: 1867
SCOTT NO. 100

Scarcity
Quantity Issued: 280,000 est.
★ Average No./Auction: .15
⊙ Average No./Auction: .51

Comments
This stamp is tightly margined. Perfs usually touch or cut one or more sides of the design. Most copies are faulty. Irregular perfs are frequently encountered and not considered a fault. Color usually appears washed-out, which is normal for this stamp. Full original gum should not be expected on unused copies, and is very scarce; never hinged copies, if they exist, are exceedingly rare. Fake grills exist.

Premium Characteristics
Sound condition, reasonably balanced margins (clear of the design, if possible), good color (to the extent possible), original gum, if unused; neat, clear cancel of the period, if used. Premium copies are almost impossible. It may be unrealistic to expect to find all the premium elements on a single stamp.

Caveats
Beware faults and repairs, including regumming and reperfing. Beware fake grills. Certificate recommended, essential for unused copies and those on cover.

90c BLUE, F Grill
YEAR OF ISSUE: 1867
SCOTT NO. 101

Scarcity
Quantity Issued: 30,000 est.
★ Average No./Auction: .22
⊙ Average No./Auction: .65

Comments
Although margins are slightly larger than other stamps of the series, perfs typically touch or cut one or more sides of the design. Irregular perfs are frequently encountered and not considered a fault. Impressions are typically crisp. Heavy cancels are commonplace on this issue; the cancels in the illustration are lighter than often encountered. Knowledgeable buyers avoid washed-out copies. Most copies are faulty. Full original gum should not be expected. Never hinged copies, if they exist, are very rare. This stamp is exceedingly rare on cover, with only one or two genuine covers and one front known. Fake grills exist.

Premium Characteristics
Sound condition, reasonably balanced margins (clear of the design, if possible), good color, original gum if unused; neat, clear (non-obliterative, if possible) cancel of the period, if used. Premium copies are difficult.

Caveats
Beware faults and repairs, including regumming and reperfing. Beware fake grills. Certificate essential for unused, unused, and copies on cover.

Note: The illustrations are intended to give an idea of the typical size of margins and the range of centering. Centering varies from good to bad on all values.

SERIES OF 1861-6 REISSUE
YEAR OF ISSUE: 1875
SCOTT NOS. 102-111

Scarcity

Quantity Issued:		★ Avg No./Auction:	
No. 102	3,195	No. 102	.38
No. 103	797	No. 103	.25
No. 104	465	No. 104	.19
No. 105	672	No. 105	.23
No. 106	451	No. 106	.26
No. 107	389	No. 107	.22
No. 108	397	No. 108	.20
No. 109	346	No. 109	.18
No. 110	346	No. 110	.20
No. 111	317	No. 111	.25

Comments
Some controversy exists over whether these stamps were issued with or without gum. They were valid for postage; used copies exist but are rare. They are more largely margined than their regularly issued counterparts due to new plates for most, and they are somewhat better centered. Nevertheless, premium copies with balanced margins are elusive, especially the 24-cent and 30-cent values, which are usually tightly margined (note the comparative size of margins in the illustration). Some contain faults, often from hinging with typical heavy hinges of the nineteenth century. Original gum, when present, is often partial or heavily hinged. Never hinged copies, if they exist, are exceedingly rare. Uneven or irregular perfs are to be expected and not considered a fault.

Premium Characteristics
Sound condition, balanced margins (clear of the design, if possible), vivid color, original gum, if unused; neat, clear, legitimate cancel, if used. Premium copies are scarce (the 24-cent and 30-cent are the most difficult).

Caveats
Beware faults and repairs, including regumming and reperfing. Beware fakes made from proofs. Certificate essential.

1c BUFF
YEAR OF ISSUE: 1869
SCOTT NO. 112

Scarcity
Quantity Issued: 16,605,150
★ Average No./Auction: .45

Comments
This stamp often has a dull, washed-out appearance, especially used. It is somewhat better margined than other

stamps of the 1869 series, still, it is not uncommon for perfs to touch or cut. Many copies are faulty. Irregular perfs are commonplace and not considered a fault. Full original gum should not be expected on unused copies; never hinged copies are scarce. The illustrated example is a premium quality copy.

Premium Characteristics
Sound condition, balanced margins (preferably large), good color, original gum if unused; neat, clear cancel of the period for used. Premium unused copies are scarce and command a substantial premium; premium used copies are surprisingly scarce, centering being the most difficult element.

Caveats
Beware faults and repairs, including regumming and reperfing. Certificate recommended for unused; essential for never hinged.

2c BROWN
YEAR OF ISSUE: 1869
SCOTT NO. 113

Scarcity
Quantity Issued: 57,387,500
★ Average No./Auction: .53

Comments
Margins are small and often hug the design. Perfs typically touch or cut

on one or more sides. Engraving is sharper than on most other values of the series. Faults are commonplace. Irregular perfs are typical and not considered a fault. Full original gum should not be expected on unused copies. Gum is typically partial or disturbed. Never hinged copies are scarce. Several collectible shades exist. The illustrated example is a gem.

Premium Characteristics
Sound condition, balanced margins (preferably large), good color, full original gum, lightly hinged or never hinged; neat, clear cancel of the period for used. Premium unused copies are very difficult; premium used copies are somewhat difficult.

Caveats
Beware faults and repairs, including regumming and reperfing. Certificate recommended for unused; essential for never hinged.

3c ULTRAMARINE
YEAR OF ISSUE: 1869
SCOTT NO. 114

Scarcity
Quantity Issued: 386,475,900
★ Average No./Auction: .48

Comments
Margins are small and often hug the design. Perfs typically touch or cut on one or more sides. Several shades exist. Freshly colored copies are more appealing. Faults are commonplace. Irregular perf are typical and not considered a fault. Full original gum should not be expected on unused copies. Gum is typically partial or disturbed. Never hinged copies are not scarce, but command a premium. Many desirable cancels are known on this issue, some of which command a substantial premium. The illustrated example is a gem.

Premium Characteristics
Sound condition, balanced margins (preferably large), fresh color, original gum, lightly hinged or never hinged; neat, clear cancel of the period for used. Premium unused copies are only moderately difficult; premium used copies are not difficult.

Caveats
Beware faults and repairs, including regumming and reperfing. Certificate recommended for unused; essential for never hinged.

6c ULTRAMARINE
YEAR OF ISSUE: 1869
SCOTT NO. 115

Scarcity
Quantity Issued: 4,882,750
★ Average No./Auction: .40
⊚ Average No./Auction: .68

Comments
Margins are small and often hug design. Perfs typically touch or cut on one or more sides. Jumbo margined copies exist, but are very scarce and command a substantial a premium. Color on this issue does not blaze and is typically understated. Faults are commonplace. Irregular perfs are typical and not considered a fault. Full original gum should not be expected on unused copies. Gum is typically partial or disturbed. Never hinged copies exist are extremely scarce. The illustrated example is nicely centered for this issue.

Premium Characteristics
Sound condition, balanced margins (preferably large), decent color, full original gum, lightly hinged or never hinged; neat, clear cancel of the period, if used. Premium copies are extremely difficult.

Caveats
Beware faults and repairs, including regumming and reperfing. Beware fakes made from rebacked, regummed, grilled proofs. Certificate recommended for original gum, essential for never hinged.

10c YELLOW
YEAR OF ISSUE: 1869
SCOTT NO. 116

Scarcity
Quantity Issued: 3,299,700
★ Average No./Auction: .62
⊚ Average No./Auction: 1.10

Comments
Margins are small and perfs typically touch or cut the design on one or more sides. Color often appears

washed out and lackluster. Deep, richly colored copies exist and are worth watching for. Used copies are often atrociously cancelled with cork killers. Faults are commonplace. Irregular perfs are typical and not considered a fault. Full original gum should not be expected on unused copies. Gum is typically partial or disturbed. Never hinged copies exist, but are extremely rare.

Premium Characteristics
Sound condition, balanced margins (preferably large), rich color, original gum, lightly hinged (or never hinged); neat, clear (and light in the case of cork killers) cancels of the period. Premium copies are difficult. The illustrated example is nicely centered for this issue.

Caveats
Beware faults and repairs, including regumming and reperfing. Beware fakes made from rebacked, regummed, grilled proofs. Certificate recommended for unused; essential for never hinged.

12c GREEN
YEAR OF ISSUE: 1869
SCOTT NO. 117

Scarcity
Quantity Issued: 3,012,950
★ Average No./Auction: .62
⊚ Average No./Auction: .91

Comments
Margins are small and often hug design. Perfs typically touch or cut on one or more sides. Jumbo margined copies exist, but are rare

and worth a substantial premium. Color is stable and not a problem, so avoid washed out copies. Faults are commonplace. Irregular perfs are typical and not considered a fault. Full original gum should not be expected on unused copies. Gum is typically partial or disturbed. Never hinged copies are very rare. The illustrated copy is beautifully margined and centered.

Premium Characteristics
Sound condition, balanced margins (preferably large), good color, full original gum, lightly hinged (if possible); neat, clear (and light in the case of cork killer) cancels of the period, if used. Premium copies are very difficult. The illustrated example is a gem as nicely centered as one could wish for.

Caveats
Beware faults and repairs, including regumming and reperfing. Beware fakes made from rebacked, regummed, grilled proofs. Certificate recommended for original gum, essential for never hinged.

15c BROWN & BLUE, Type I
YEAR OF ISSUE: 1869
SCOTT NO. 118

Scarcity
Quantity Issued: 200,000 est.
★ Average No./Auction: .33
⊙ Average No./Auction: .72

Comments
Perfs typically touch or cut on one or more sides. Jumbo margined copies

exist but are very rare. The illustrated example is a gem. Copies with strong, rich colors are prized. Used copies are often obliterated with cork killers. Faults are commonplace. Irregular perfs are typical and not considered a fault. Full original gum should not be expected on unused copies. Gum is typically partial or disturbed. Never hinged copies are exceedingly rare.

Premium Characteristics
Sound condition, balanced margins (preferably large), rich color, original gum, lightly hinged (if possible); neat, clear (and light in the case of cork killer) cancel of the period. Premium copies are extremely difficult.

Caveats
Beware faults and repairs, including regumming and reperfing. Beware fakes made from rebacked, regummed, grilled proofs. Certificate recommended for unused; essential for never hinged.

15c BROWN & BLUE, Type II
YEAR OF ISSUE: 1869
SCOTT NO. 119

Scarcity
Quantity Issued: 1,238,000 est.
★ Average No./Auction: .49
⊙ Average No./Auction: .82

Comments
Perfs typically touch or cut on one or more sides. Jumbo margined copies

exist but are very rare. Copies with strong, rich colors are prized. Used copies are often obliterated with cork killers. Faults are commonplace. Irregular perfs are typical and not considered a fault. Full original gum should not be expected on unused copies. Gum is typically partial or disturbed. Never hinged copies are very rare. The illustrated example is nicer than usually encountered.

Premium Characteristics
Sound condition, balanced margins (preferably large), rich color, original gum, lightly hinged (if possible); neat, clear (and light in the case of cork killer) cancel of the period. Premium copies are extremely difficult.

Caveats
Beware faults and repairs, including regumming and reperfing. Beware fakes made from rebacked, regummed, grilled proofs. Certificate recommended for original gum, essential for never hinged.

24c GREEN & VIOLET
YEAR OF ISSUE: 1869
SCOTT NO. 120

Scarcity
Quantity Issued: 235,350
★ Average No./Auction: .59
⊙ Average No./Auction: .92

Comments
Perfs typically touch or cut on one or more sides. Jumbo margined copies exist but are very rare. Visually

appealing used copies are difficult because of the stamp's color and typical heavy cork killer cancels. Faults are commonplace. Irregular perfs are typical and not considered a fault. Full original gum should not be expected on unused copies. Gum is typically partial or disturbed. Never hinged copies are exceedingly rare. The illustrated example is a wonderfully centered gem of uncommon quality.

Premium Characteristics
Sound condition, balanced margins (preferably large), good color, original gum, lightly hinged (if possible); neat, clear (and light in the case of cork killer) cancel of the period, if used. Premium copies are extremely difficult.

Caveats
Beware faults and repairs, including regumming and reperfing. Beware fakes made from rebacked, regummed, grilled proofs. Certificate recommended for unused; essential for never hinged and for copies on cover.

30c BLUE & CARMINE
YEAR OF ISSUE: 1869
SCOTT NO. 121

Scarcity
Quantity Issued: 244,1100
★ Average No./Auction: .54
⊙ Average No./Auction: 1.10

Comments
Perfs typically touch or cut on one or more sides. Jumbo margined copies exist but are very rare. Often appears washed out; those with

strong, rich colors are prized. The illustrated example is a gem. Used copies typically obliterated with cork killers. Faults are commonplace. Irregular perfs are typical and not considered a fault. Full original gum should not be expected on unused copies. Gum is typically partial or disturbed. Never hinged copies, if they exist, are exceedingly rare.

Premium Characteristics
Sound condition, balanced margins (preferably large), rich color, original gum, lightly hinged (if possible); neat, clear (and light in the case of cork killer) cancel of the period, if used. Premium copies are extremely difficult.

Caveats
Beware faults and repairs, including regumming and reperfing. Beware fakes made from rebacked, regummed, grilled proofs. Certificate recommended for original gum, essential for never hinged and for copies on cover.

90c CARMINE & BLACK
YEAR OF ISSUE: 1869
SCOTT NO. 122

Scarcity
Quantity Issued: 47,460
★ Average No./Auction: .65
⊙ Average No./Auction: .90

Comments
Perfs typically touch or cut on one or more sides. Margins tend to be small. Large margined copies exist but are very rare. Nicely centered copies are difficult. The illustrated example is a wonderfully centered gem of uncommonly high quality. Colors and impression usually more distinct than on others of the 1869 series. Used copies typically obliterated with cork killers. Faults are commonplace. Irregular perfs are typical and not considered a fault. Full original gum should not be expected on unused copies. Gum is typically partial or disturbed. Never hinged copies, if they exist, would be of the utmost rarity. One copy of this stamp is known used on cover.

Premium Characteristics
Sound condition, balanced margins (preferably large), good color, original gum, lightly hinged (if possible); neat, clear (and light in the case of cork killer) cancel of the period, if used. Premium copies are extremely difficult.

Caveats
Beware faults and repairs, including regumming and reperfing. Beware fakes made from rebacked, regummed, grilled proofs. Certificate recommended for unused; essential for never hinged or stamp on cover.

1c BUFF, RE-ISSUE OF 1880
YEAR OF ISSUE: 1880
SCOTT NO. 133

Scarcity
Quantity Issued:
★ Average No./Auction: .29
⊙ Average No./Auction: .09

Comments
Issued on soft porous paper without grill. Exists in two shades: buff, issued with gum; and orange brown, issued without gum. Never hinged copies of the buff shade exist, but are very rare. Less difficult to find in visually appealing condition than Scott No. 112, but, nevertheless, scarce. Irregular perfs are frequently encountered and not considered a fault.

Premium Characteristics
Sound condition, balanced margins, good color, lightly hinged original gum (if appropriate); neat, clear cancel of the period for used, if used. Premium copies are less difficult than on the regularly issued stamp.

Caveats
Beware faults and repairs. Certificate strongly recommended.

SERIES OF 1869
(Scott Nos. 112-122)

Examples of the 1869 issue illustrating typical margins, centering, and perforations.

1869 ISSUE, REISSUE OF 1875
YEAR OF ISSUE: 1875
SCOTT NOS. 123-132

Scarcity
Quantity Issued:

No. 123	(1c)	8,252
No. 124	(2c)	4,755
No. 125	(3c)	1,406
No. 126	(6c)	2,226
No. 127	(10c)	1,947
No. 128	(12c)	1,584
No. 129	(15c)	1,981
No. 130	(24c)	2,091
No. 131	(30c)	1,535
No. 132	(90c)	1,536

Average No./Auction:

	Unused	Used
No. 123	.36	.14
No. 124	.31	.12
No. 125	.34	n/a
No. 126	.41	.16
No. 127	.34	.14
No. 128	.25	.07
No. 129	.55	.21
No. 130	.44	.10
No. 131	.51	.10
No. 132	.51	.11

Comments
Issued on hard white paper without grills. Traditionally regarded as having been issued with white, crackly gum (although some controversy exists as to whether they were issued with or without gum). Typically poorly centered. Large margined copies are scarce, especially the 3-cent value. The 6c-90c values are more frequently encountered with large margins than their regularly issued counterparts (Scott Nos. 115-122). Colors are brighter and deeper than on the regular issue. The 30-cent especially displays more pronounced color. The engraving on the reissued stamps appears sharper. Used copes of the higher values are often obliterated by heavy, 1875-type cancels. This issue is plagued by faults, short perfs, and reperfing. Gum is typically partial or disturbed. Never hinged copies, if they exist, are extremely rare. Only a few authentic used copies of Scott No. 125 are known.

Premium Characteristics
Sound condition, balanced margins (preferably large), rich color, original gum, lightly hinged (if possible); neat, clear cancel of the period for used. Premium copies are extremely difficult.

Caveats
Beware faults and repairs, including regumming and reperfing. Beware fakes made from proofs. Beware stamps of the regular issue with ironed out grills offered as reissues. Certificate essential.

Examples of the 1869 reissue illustrating margins, centering, and perforations typical of the series.

NATIONAL BANK NOTE ISSUE OF 1870
WITH GRILLS (Scott Nos. 134-144)

General characteristics of the series are given below. Characteristics unique to a specific stamp are given under that stamp's listing.

General Comments
Typically poorly centered. Copies with balanced margins are difficult, especially unused. Tends to be small margined; perforations often touch or cut design on at least one side. Faults are commonplace. The hard paper Nationals are less prone to thinning than the later soft paper banknotes, however, the hard paper is susceptible to tears and creases. Irregular perfs are typical, in fact, to be expected, and not considered a fault. The paper used to print Nationals was rather tough and not prone to separate cleanly, hence the usual "rough" perfs. Gum is usually partial or disturbed. This series is the most difficult of the banknotes. Premium copies are very elusive and command substantial premiums. It is almost impossible to find all the premium elements in a single stamp.

Grills
Grills on this issue are often faint or partially impressed. Clearly impressed grills command a premium; full, strongly impressed grills command a substantial premium. Grills on the Nationals are frequently faked. Fake grills are usually uncharacteristically complete or strong. Knowledgeable buyers tend to regard uncharacteristically pronounced grills with caution. Collectors should not be overly selective about the condition of grills on this issue, bearing in mind that a faint or partially impressed grill is standard.

Illustrations appearing with each stamp's listing are intended to give a general idea of quality, margins, centering, perforations, and cancels. They are neither the best nor worst examples of a given denomination. Nationals of superlative quality, such as those illustrated below, are rare, highly prized, and expensive, when, indeed, they can be found.

A sampling of truly gem quality grilled Nationals.

1c ULTRAMARINE
YEAR OF ISSUE: 1870
SCOTT NO. 134

Scarcity
Quantity Issued: 5,000,000 est.
★ Average No./Auction: .14

Comments
Refer to the general comments on page 55. Color often appears washed out and lacks luster. Grills are often faint. Never hinged copies exist, but are rare. Fake grills exist.

Premium Characteristics
Sound condition, balanced margins, good color, reasonably impressed grill, original gum, lightly hinged (or never hinged); neat, clear cancel for the period, if used. Premium copies are difficult, especially unused.

Caveats
Beware faults and repairs, including regumming and reperfing. Beware fake grills. Certificate recommended for unused copies; essential for never hinged.

2c RED BROWN
YEAR OF ISSUE: 1870
SCOTT NO. 135

Scarcity
Quantity Issued: 10,000,000 est.
★ Average No./Auction: .34

Comments
Refer to the general comments on page 55. This stamp is not known for being boldly colored. Never hinged copies exist, but are rare. Fake grills exist.

Premium Characteristics
Sound condition, balanced margins, good color, reasonably impressed grill, full original gum, lightly hinged (if possible); neat, clear cancel for period, if used. Premium copies are difficult, especially unused.

Caveats
Beware faults and repairs, including regumming and reperfing. Beware fake grills. Certificate recommended for unused copies, essential never hinged.

3c GREEN
YEAR OF ISSUE: 1870
SCOTT NO. 136

Scarcity
Quantity Issued: 50,000,000 est.
★ Average No./Auction: .33

Comments
Refer to the general comments on page 55. Unused copies with balanced margins are difficult, however, used copies exist in sufficient numbers to make them less difficult. Color is typically much lighter than later 3-cent banknotes.

Never hinged copies exist, but are scarce. Some copies are lightly grilled and grill is difficult to detect. Three-cent grills are not frequently faked, however, fakes do exist.

Premium Characteristics
Sound condition, balanced margins, good color, original gum, lightly hinged (or never hinged); neat, clear cancel of the period, if used. Premium unused copies are difficult.

Caveats
Beware faults and repairs, including regumming and reperfing. Beware fake grills. Certificate recommended for unused copies; essential for never hinged.

6c CARMINE
YEAR OF ISSUE: 1870
SCOTT NO. 137

Scarcity
Quantity Issued: 400,000 est.
★ Average No./Auction: .34
⊙ Average No./Auction: .47

Comments
Refer to the general comments on page 55. Richly colored copies are desirable. Never hinged copies are very rare. Grills are often faint and difficult to detect. Dangerous fake grills exist.

Premium Characteristics
Sound condition, balanced margins, good color, reasonably impressed grill, full original gum, lightly hinged (if possible); neat, clear cancel of the period, if used. Premium copies are difficult, especially unused and command substantial premiums.

Caveats
Beware faults and repairs, including regumming and reperfing. Beware fake grills. Certificate strongly recommended, essential for never hinged.

7c VERMILION
YEAR OF ISSUE: 1871
SCOTT NO. 138

Scarcity
Quantity Issued: 120,000 est.
★ Average No./Auction: .13
⊙ Average No./Auction: .59

Comments
Refer to the general comments on page 55. This stamp is small margined and typically poorly centered. It is very scarce unused. Never hinged copies, if they exist, are rare. Some copies are lightly grilled and the grill is difficult to detect. Dangerous counterfeit grills exist.

Premium Characteristics
Sound condition, balanced margins, good color, reasonably impressed grill, original gum, lightly hinged; neat, clear cancel of the period, if used. Premium unused copies are very difficult and worth substantial premiums.

Caveats
Beware faults and repairs, including regumming and reperfing. Beware fake grills. Certificate recommended, essential for never hinged.

10c BROWN
YEAR OF ISSUE: 1870
SCOTT NO. 139

Scarcity
Quantity Issued: 80,000 est.
★ Average No./Auction: .34
⊙ Average No./Auction: .47

Comments
Refer to the general comments on page 55. The engraved impression is typically crisp, if somewhat lightly inked. Never hinged copies, if they exist, are rare. Grills are notoriously faint and difficult to detect on this value. Dangerous counterfeit grills exist.

Premium Characteristics
Sound condition, balanced margins, good color, reasonably impressed grill, full original gum, lightly hinged (if possible); neat, clear cancel of the period, if used. Premium copies are very difficult, especially unused, and command a substantial premium.

Caveats
Beware faults and repairs, including regumming and reperfing. Beware fake grills. Certificate strongly recommended, essential for never hinged.

12c DULL VIOLET
YEAR OF ISSUE: 1870
SCOTT NO. 140

Scarcity
Quantity Issued: 10,000 est.
★ Average No./Auction: .18
⊚ Average No./Auction: .34

Comments
Refer to the general comments on page 55. This stamp is extremely rare unused, and most copies are poorly centered. Color ranges from a dull or murky appearance to faded out. Faults are endemic. Never hinged copies, if they exist (which is doubtful), are of the utmost rarity. Genuine grills are usually faint. Dangerous counterfeit grills exist.

Premium Characteristics
Sound condition, balanced margins (terribly difficult to locate), good color, reasonably impressed grill, original gum; neat, clear cancels of the period, if used. Premium unused copies are exceedingly rare; the population is too restricted to permit selectivity in the normal sense. Premium used copies are very difficult.

Caveats
Beware faults and repairs, including regumming and reperfing. Beware fake grills. Certificate absolutely essential.

15c ORANGE
YEAR OF ISSUE: 1870
SCOTT NO. 141

Scarcity
Quantity Issued: 80,000 est.
★ Average No./Auction: .18
⊚ Average No./Auction: .44

Comments
Refer to the general comments on page 55. Color is typically brighter, fresher appearing than on other values of the series. Never hinged copies, if they exist, are rare. Grills are often faintly impressed, but strongly impressed grills do exist. Dangerous fake grills exist.

Premium Characteristics
Sound condition, balanced margins good color, reasonably impressed grill, full original gum, lightly hinged (if possible); neat, clear cancel of the period, if used. Premium unused copies are very difficult; premium used copies are difficult.

Caveats
Beware faults and repairs, including regumming and reperfing. Beware fake grills. Certificate strongly recommended.

Comments
This stamp is of the greatest rarity unused, with only one or two copies reported (none appeared in the auction survey). Used copies are also rare and usually poorly centered; copies with balanced margins are virtually impossible. The engraving lacks definition and contrast, and the color appears washed out. The stamp invariably looks terrible. Faults are the norm. Irregular perfs are typical and not considered a fault. Counterfeit grills abound, many dangerous.

24c PURPLE
YEAR OF ISSUE: 1870
SCOTT NO. 142

Premium Characteristics
The rarity of this stamp does not permit selectivity in the normal sense.

Scarcity
Quantity Issued: 2,000 est.
★ Average No./Auction: .00
⊘ Average No./Auction: .11

Caveats
Beware faults and repairs, including regumming and reperfing. Beware fake grills. Certificate absolutely essential.

30c BLACK
YEAR OF ISSUE: 1870
SCOTT NO. 143

Scarcity
Quantity Issued: 20,000 est.
★ Average No./Auction: .19
⊘ Average No./Auction: .31

Comments
Refer to the general comments on page 55. Engraving is more crisp and well defined on this value, and the color always intense. Never hinged

copies, if they exist, are very rare. Genuine grills are often faintly impressed. Dangerous counterfeit grills exist.

Premium Characteristics
This is one of those issues whose typical condition is so poor that any sound, reasonably attractive copy should be considered collectible.

Caveats
Beware faults and repairs, including regumming and reperfing. Beware fake grills. Certificate essential.

90c CARMINE
YEAR OF ISSUE: 1870
SCOTT NO. 144

Scarcity
Quantity Issued: 28,000 est.
★ Average No./Auction: .18
⊚ Average No./Auction: .37

Comments
Refer to the general comments on
page 55. Never hinged copies, if
they exist, are exceedingly rare.

Genuine grills are often faintly impressed.
Dangerous counterfeit grills exist.

Premium Characteristics
This is one of those issues whose typical
condition is so poor that any sound,
reasonably attractive copy should be
considered collectible.

Caveats
Beware faults and repairs, including
regumming and reperfing. Beware fake grills.
Certificate essential.

A NOTE ON CONDITION

Nineteenth century stamps are typically poorly centered, lack gum, are heavily canceled, or are
otherwise visually unappealing when compared to modern stamps. Never hinged copies are
quite uncommon and, in some cases, nonexistent. Gum, when present, is often disturbed or
partially missing, the result of heavy paper hinges, which were customary at the time.
Knowledgeable buyers are aware that the condition of gum on early stamps is typically poor and
do not have unrealistic expectations. Faults (including repairs and "improvements" such as
regumming or reperfing) are as common as tumbleweeds on the prairie.

As a general rule, any sound, reasonably centered stamp (within the limitations of the issue),
possessing good color for the issue, and a neat, clear cancel contemporaneous to the issue, if
used, is collectible. The presence of one or more premium characteristics, such as large,
balanced margins, light hinging (or never hinged), fresh, vivid color, is desirable, however, it is
extremely difficult—and sometimes impossible—to find a stamp possessing all the premium
characteristics. Superlative gem copies, when available, command substantial premiums—often
multiples of catalogue.

NATIONAL BANK NOTE ISSUE OF 1870
WITHOUT GRILLS (Scott Nos. 145-155)

General characteristics of the series are given below. Characteristics unique to a specific stamp are given under that stamp's listing.

General Comments
Typically poorly centered. Copies with balanced margins are difficult, especially unused. Margins vary from small to large, however, perforations often touch or cut design on at least one side. Faults are commonplace. The hard paper Nationals are less prone to thinning than the later soft paper banknotes, however, the hard paper is susceptible to tears and creases. Irregular perfs are typical, in fact, to be expected, and not considered a fault. The paper used to print Nationals was rather tough and not prone to separating cleanly, hence the usual "rough" perfs. Gum is usually partial or disturbed. Stamps of this series are generally more plentiful than their grilled counterparts, however, premium unused copies are still elusive and command a substantial premium. It is very difficult to find all the premium elements in a single stamp.

Illustrations appearing with each stamp's listing are intended to give a general idea of quality, margins, centering, perforations, and cancels. They are neither the best nor worst examples of a given denomination. Nationals of superlative quality, are truly scarce, highly prized, and expensive, when, indeed, they can be found.

1c ULTRAMARINE, w/o GRILL
YEAR OF ISSUE: 1870
SCOTT NO. 145

Scarcity
Quantity Issued: 140,000,000 est.
★ Average No./Auction: .24

Comments
Refer to the general comments above. Design often appears dull and washed out; rich, brightly colored copies are worth a premium. Never hinged copies exist, but are scarce.

Premium Characteristics
Sound condition, balanced margins, bright color, full original gum (lightly hinged, if possible); neat, clear cancel of the period, if used. Premium unused copies are difficult; premium used copies are available

Caveats
Beware faults and repairs, including regumming and reperfing. Certificate recommended for never hinged copies.

2c RED BROWN, w/o GRILL
YEAR OF ISSUE: 1870
SCOTT NO. 146

Scarcity
Quantity Issued: 250,000,000 est.
★ Average No./Auction: .18

Comments
Refer to the general comments on page 62. This stamp is scarcer than generally thought. Unused copies with balanced margins are uncommon. Color is typically solid; impression well defined. Never hinged copies exist, but are relatively scarce.

Premium Characteristics
Sound condition, balanced margins, good color, full original gum, lightly hinged (if possible); neat, clear cancel of the period, if used. Premium unused copies are scarce.

Caveats
Beware faults and repairs, including regumming and reperfing. Certificate recommended for never hinged copies.

3c GREEN, w/o GRILL
YEAR OF ISSUE: 1870
SCOTT NO. 147

Scarcity
Quantity Issued: 1,200,000,000 est.
★ Average No./Auction: .40

Comments
Refer to the general comments on page 62. The large population of this stamp makes finding premium copies less difficult. Used copies are abundant. Impressions are crisp.

Never hinged copies exist, and are only relatively scarce.

Premium Characteristics
Sound condition, large balanced margins, fresh color, original gum, lightly hinged (or never hinged); neat, clear cancel of the period, if used. Premium unused copies are somewhat difficult.

Caveats
Beware faults and repairs, including regumming and reperfing. Certificate recommended for never hinged copies.

6c CARMINE, w/o GRILL
YEAR OF ISSUE: 1870
SCOTT NO. 148

Scarcity
Quantity Issued: 27,600,000 est.
★ Average No./Auction: .25

Comments
Refer to the general comments on page 62. Color and impression typically solid. Never hinged copies are very scarce.

Premium Characteristics
Sound condition, balanced margins, good color, full original gum, lightly hinged (if possible); neat, clear cancel for the period, if used. Premium unused copies are difficult.

Caveats
Beware faults and repairs, including regumming and reperfing. Certificate strongly recommended; essential for never hinged.

7c VERMILION, w/o GRILL
YEAR OF ISSUE: 1871
SCOTT NO. 149

Scarcity
Quantity Issued: 2,825,000 est.
★ Average No./Auction: .23

Comments
Refer to the general comments on page 62. Although this stamp is frequently better margined than other values of the series, nicely centered, large margined copies are still the exception rather than the rule. Never hinged copies are very scarce.

Premium Characteristics
Sound condition, balanced margins, good color, original gum, lightly hinged; neat, clear cancel of the period, if used. Premium unused copies are very difficult.

Caveats
Beware faults and repairs, including regumming and reperfing. Certificate recommended for never hinged copies.

10c BROWN, w/o GRILL
YEAR OF ISSUE: 1870
SCOTT NO. 150

Scarcity
Quantity Issued: 10,920,000 est.
★ Average No./Auction: .12

Comments
Refer to the general comments on page 62. Never hinged copies are rare.

Premium Characteristics
Sound condition, large balanced margins, good color, full original gum, lightly hinged; neat, clear cancel of the period, if used. Premium unused copies are very difficult.

Caveats
Beware faults and repairs, including regumming and reperfing. Certificate recommended for never hinged copies.

12c DULL VIOLET, w/o GRILL
YEAR OF ISSUE: 1870
SCOTT NO. 151

Scarcity
Quantity Issued: 3,890,000 est.
★ Average No./Auction: .30

Comments
Refer to the general comments on page 62. Most copies are poorly centered. Color typically appears faded or washed out. R.H. White suggests that the pigment may be susceptible to certain watermark

fluids. Never hinged copies are very rare.

Premium Characteristics
Sound condition, balanced margins, good color (to the extent possible), original gum; neat clear cancel of the period, if used. Premium used copies are difficult; premium unused copies are exceedingly difficult.

Caveats
Beware faults and repairs, including regumming and reperfing. Certificate recommended; essential for never hinged copies.

15c BRIGHT ORANGE, w/o GRILL
YEAR OF ISSUE: 1870
SCOTT NO. 152

Scarcity
Quantity Issued: 5,500,000 est.
★ Average No./Auction: .24

Comments
Refer to the general comments on page 62. Copies with balanced margins are difficult, especially unused. Color and definition typically better than on other values of the series. Never hinged copies are very rare.

Premium Characteristics
Sound condition, balanced margins, good color, full original gum, lightly hinged (if possible); neat, clear cancel of the period, if used. Premium copies are incredibly difficult.

Caveats
Beware faults and repairs, including regumming and reperfing. Certificate recommended; essential for never hinged copies.

24c PURPLE, w/o GRILL
YEAR OF ISSUE: 1870
SCOTT NO. 153

Scarcity
Quantity Issued: 1,148,000 est.
★ Average No./Auction: .49

Comments
Refer to the general comments on page 62. The engraving lacks definition and contrast, and the stamp is notoriously poorly colored, often with a washed out appearance. Never hinged copies are very rare.

Premium Characteristics
This is one of those issues whose typical condition is so poor that any sound, reasonably attractive copy can be considered collectible. Premium copies, unused or used, command huge premiums over catalogue.

Caveats
Beware faults and repairs, including regumming and reperfing. Certificate recommended, including copies on cover; essential for premium copies.

30c BLACK, w/o GRILL
YEAR OF ISSUE: 1870
SCOTT NO. 154

Scarcity
Quantity Issued: 893,000 est.
★ Average No./Auction: .26

Comments
Refer to the general comments on page 62. Copies with balanced margins are difficult, large margins are especially difficult. Engraving is sharp and crisp on this value. Never hinged copies may exist, but are very rare.

Premium Characteristics
Sound condition, balanced margins, good color (deep black color is especially prized), full original gum (lightly hinged, if possible); neat, clear cancel of the period, if used. Premium copies are very difficult.

Caveats
Beware faults and repairs, including regumming and reperfing. Certificate recommended for unused copies; essential for never hinged copies.

90c CARMINE, w/o GRILL
YEAR OF ISSUE: 1870
SCOTT NO. 155

Scarcity
Quantity Issued: 185,000 est.
★ Average No./Auction: .23
⊘ Average No./Auction: .56

Comments
Refer to the general comments on page 62. Often poorly centered. Color is fairly uniform; faded copies are avoided by knowledgeable buyers. Never hinged copies, if they exist, are very rare.

Premium Characteristics
Sound condition, balanced margins, good color, full original gum (lightly hinged, if possible); neat, clear cancel of the period, if used. Premium copies are very difficult.

Caveats
Beware faults and repairs, including regumming and reperfing. Certificate recommended, and essential for never hinged copies or copies on cover.

CONTINENTAL BANK NOTE ISSUE OF 1873
(Scott Nos. 156-166)

General characteristics of the series are given below. Characteristics unique to a specific stamp are given under that stamp's listing. Used stamps of nominal or moderate value were not surveyed at auction.

General Comments
Typically poorly centered. Copies with balanced margins are difficult, especially unused. Margins vary from small to large, however, perforations often touch or cut design on at least one side. Faults are commonplace. The paper used on Continentals is less prone to thinning than the later soft paper banknotes, however, the hard paper is susceptible to tears and creases. Irregular perfs are typical, in fact, to be expected, and not considered a fault. Gum is usually partial or disturbed. Premium unused copies are fairly difficult to locate and command a substantial premium, when available. Many interesting and value enhancing cancels can be found on Continentals.

Premium Characteristics
Sound condition, balanced margins, fresh color, lightly hinged (or never hinged) original gum; neat, clear cancel of the period, if used. It is not always possible to find never hinged copies, especially the rare items. It is very difficult to find all premium elements in a single stamp.

The illustration appearing with each stamp's listing in this section is purely for convenience. The range of centering, typical size of margins, and condition of perforation on Continentals is similar to that found on the preceding National issue. Refer to illustrations appearing with those listings for a general idea.

1c ULTRAMARINE
YEAR OF ISSUE: 1873
SCOTT NO. 156

Scarcity
Quantity Issued: 780,000,000 est.
★ Average No./Auction: .13

Comments
Refer to the general comments

above. Many shades exist from pale ultramarine to rich, dark blues. However, color is typically paler, less vivid than on preceding 1-cent banknotes. Never hinged copies exist, but are scarce. Because this stamp is relatively plentiful, premium copies are less difficult than higher denominations. Generally speaking, regard imperforate singles as bogus.

Premium Characteristics
Refer to the comments at the top of the page. Premium unused copies are relatively scarce; premium used copies are available.

Caveats
Beware faults and repairs, including regumming and reperfing. Certificate recommended for never hinged copies.

2c BROWN
YEAR OF ISSUE: 1873
SCOTT NO. 157

Scarcity
Quantity Issued: 112,500,000 est.
★ Average No./Auction: .33

Comments
Refer to the general comments on page 68.
Exists in a variety of shades. Never hinged
copies exist, but are relatively scarce.

Premium Characteristics
Refer to the comments on page 68. Premium
unused copies are relatively scarce; premium
used copies are available.

Caveats
Beware faults and repairs, including
regumming and reperfing. Certificate
recommended for never hinged copies.

3c GREEN
YEAR OF ISSUE: 1873
SCOTT NO. 158

Scarcity
Quantity Issued: 2,610,000,000 est.
★ Average No./Auction: .29

Comments
Refer to the general comments on page 68.
This stamp's large population makes finding
premium copies less difficult. Used copies
are abundant. Never hinged copies exist,
and although they are not common, neither
are they scarce.

Premium Characteristics
Refer to the comments on page 68. Premium
unused copies are not difficult.

Caveats
Beware faults and repairs, including
regumming and reperfing.

6c DULL PINK
YEAR OF ISSUE: 1873
SCOTT NO. 159

Scarcity
Quantity Issued: 47,000,000 est.
★ Average No./Auction: .35

Comments
Refer to the general comments on page 68.
Color is typically washed out, and appears
faded when compared to the previous the
National issue. Many worthwhile cancels
exists on this issue, including an especially
wide variety of New York foreign mails.
Never hinged copies are scarce.

Premium Characteristics
Refer to the comments on page 68. Premium
unused copies are difficult.

Caveats
Beware faults and repairs, including
regumming and reperfing. Certificate
recommended for unused, essential for never
hinged.

7c ORANGE VERMILION
YEAR OF ISSUE: 1873
SCOTT NO. 160

Scarcity
Quantity Issued: 2,500,000 est.
★ Average No./Auction: .28

Comments
Refer to the general comments on page 68.
Never hinged copies are very rare. Many
nice New York foreign mail cancels exist on
this value.

Premium Characteristics
Refer to the comments on page 68. Premium
unused copies are very difficult.

Caveats
Beware faults and repairs, including
regumming and reperfing. Certificate
recommended for never hinged copies.

10c BROWN
YEAR OF ISSUE: 1873
SCOTT NO. 161

Scarcity
Quantity Issued: 30,000,000 est.
★ Average No./Auction: .21

Comments
Refer to the general comments on page 68.
Never hinged copies are rare. Many nice
New York foreign mail cancels exist on this
value.

Premium Characteristics
Refer to the comments on page 68. Premium
unused copies are difficult.

Caveats
Beware faults and repairs, including
regumming and reperfing. Beware removed
pen cancels. Certificate recommended for
never hinged copies.

12c BLACKISH VIOLET
YEAR OF ISSUE: 1873
SCOTT NO. 162

Scarcity
Quantity Issued: 2,915,000 est.
★ Average No./Auction: .35

Comments
Refer to the general comments on page 68.
Color usually darker, not as faded as the
National printing. Fresh, intensely colored
copies are prized by knowledgeable buyers.
Never hinged copies are very rare. Many
nice New York foreign mail cancels exist on
this value.

Premium Characteristics
Refer to the comments on page 68. Intense
color. Premium unused copies are very
difficult; premium used copies are difficult;

Caveats
Beware faults and repairs, including
regumming and reperfing. Certificate
recommended, especially for never hinged
copies.

Comments
Refer to the general comments on page 68. Exists in several shades. Never hinged copies are very rare.

Premium Characteristics
This stamp is rarely encountered in premium condition, either unused or used.

15c YELLOW ORANGE
YEAR OF ISSUE: 1873
SCOTT NO. 163

Caveats
Beware faults and repairs, including regumming and reperfing. Certificate recommended for never hinged copies.

Scarcity
Quantity Issued: 5,500,000 est.
★ Average No./Auction: .13

Comments
Refer to the general comments on page 68. Exists in several collectible shades. Never hinged copies are very rare.

Premium Characteristics
Refer to the comments on page 68. Premium copies are very difficult.

30c GRAY BLACK
YEAR OF ISSUE: 1873
SCOTT NO. 165

Caveats
Beware faults and repairs, including regumming and reperfing. Certificate recommended, essential for never hinged.

Scarcity
Quantity Issued: 2,050,000 est.
★ Average No./Auction: .34

Comments
Refer to the general comments on page 68. Never hinged copies are very rare.

Premium Characteristics
Refer to the comments on page 68. Good color. Premium copies are very difficult.

Caveats
Beware faults and repairs, including regumming and reperfing. Because this issue is so difficult to distinguish from the National printing, certificate is recommended. Certificate essential for copies on cover.

90c CARMINE
YEAR OF ISSUE: 1873
SCOTT NO. 166

Scarcity
Quantity Issued: 197,000 est.
★ Average No./Auction: .56
⊚ Average No./Auction: .52

SERIES OF 1873
SPECIAL PRINTING OF 1875
SCOTT NOS. 167-77, 180-1

Scarcity
Quantity Issued:
Note: The Post Office did not keep separate records for the quantities sold of the 1875 and 1880 special printings. The combined quantities are listed below.

Nos. 167 & 192	(1c)	388
Nos. 168 & 193	(2c)	416
Nos. 169 & 194	(3c)	267
Nos. 170 & 195	(6c)	185
Nos. 171 & 196	(7c)	473
Nos. 172 & 197	(10c)	180
Nos. 173 & 198	(12c)	282
Nos. 174 & 199	(15c)	169
Nos. 175 & 200	(24c)	286
Nos. 176 & 201	(30c)	179
Nos. 177 & 202	(90c)	170
Nos. 180 & 203	(2c)	917
Nos. 181 & 204	(5c)	317

★ Average No./Auction:

No. 167	.04
No. 168	.06
No. 169	.04
No. 170	.04
No. 171	.06
No. 172	.07
No. 173	.10
No. 174	.04
No. 175	.08
No. 176	.03
No. 177	.02
No. 180	.01
No. 181	.00

Comments
Issued without gum on hard white paper. They were valid for postage. With the exception of the 3-cent value, used copies are not generally known to exist. These stamps were usually separated by scissors. Copies without scissors cuts are known but are exceedingly rare and prized. Perforations are often missing on one or more sides. Copies without cuts into the their designs are more desirable. Many contain faults (scissors cuts are not considered a fault), often from hinging with typical heavy hinges of the nineteenth century.

Although the quantities sold for the 1875 and 1880 special printings are combined, the latter issue is much scarcer. Also, the 2-cent carmine vermilion/scarlet vermilion is much rarer that the figures indicate. No copies of Scott No. 181, the 5-cent bright blue, appeared at auction in the survey.

Premium Characteristics
Copies without faults. Copies with scissors cuts clear of the design (copies without any scissors cuts at all are highly prized). Stamps of this issue are very difficult to locate in any condition. Buyers should not have unreasonably high expectations of quality when considering this issue.

Caveats
Beware faults and repairs, especially improved perforations. Certificate essential.

Examples illustrating typical scissors cut separation.

2c VERMILION
YEAR OF ISSUE: 1875
SCOTT NO. 178

Scarcity
Quantity Issued: 279,000,000 est.
★ Average No./Auction: .25

Comments
Refer to the general comments on page 68.
Many shades exist. Never hinged copies are
scarce.

Premium Characteristics
Refer to the comments on page 68. Premium
unused copies are difficult.

Caveats
Beware faults and repairs, including
regumming and reperfing. Certificate
recommended; essential for never hinged.

5c BLUE
YEAR OF ISSUE: 1875
SCOTT NO. 179

Scarcity
Quantity Issued: 38,000,000 est.
★ Average No./Auction: .26

Comments
Refer to the general comments on page 68.
Never hinged copies are scarce.

Premium Characteristics
Refer to the comments on page 68. Premium
copies are difficult.

Caveats
Beware faults and repairs, including
regumming and reperfing. Certificate
recommended for never hinged.

Examples of gem quality Continental Bank Note issues.

AMERICAN BANK NOTE ISSUE OF 1879
(Scott Nos. 182-191)

General characteristics of the series are given below. Characteristics unique to a specific stamp are given under that stamp's listing. Used stamps of nominal or moderate value were not surveyed at auction.

General Comments
Typically poorly centered. Margins vary from small to large, however, perforations often touch or cut design on at least one side. Copies with balanced margins are difficult, especially unused. Faults are commonplace. The soft porous paper used for this issue is prone to thinning, especially from the removal of heavy nineteenth century hinges. Irregular perfs are frequently encountered, but typically are not as pronounced as on the hard paper issues; they are not considered a fault. Gum is usually partial or disturbed. Premium unused copies are fairly difficult to locate and command a substantial premium when available.

Premium Characteristics
Sound condition, balanced margins, fresh color, lightly hinged (or never hinged) original gum; neat, clear cancel of the period, if used. It is not always possible to find never hinged copies, especially for the higher values. It is very difficult to find all premium elements in a single stamp.

The illustration appearing with each stamp's listing in this section is purely for convenience. The range of centering and typical size of margins is similar to other banknote issues.

1c DARK ULTRAMARINE
YEAR OF ISSUE: 1879
SCOTT NO. 182

Scarcity
Quantity Issued: 590,000,000 est.
★ Average No./Auction: .22

Comments
Refer to the general comments above. This stamp exists in a wide range of shades. Vividly colored copies are especially prized. Never hinged copies are available, but not common.

Premium Characteristics
Refer to the comments at the top of this page. Premium unused copies are relatively scarce. This stamp is plentiful in used condition; premium used copies are not difficult.

Caveats
Beware faults and repairs, including regumming and reperfing. Certificate recommended for never hinged copies.

2c VERMILION
YEAR OF ISSUE: 1879
SCOTT NO. 183

Scarcity
Quantity Issued: 440,000,000 est.
★ Average No./Auction: .28

Comments
Refer to the general comments on page 74.
Never hinged copies are not scarce.

Premium Characteristics
Refer to the comments on page 74.
Premium unused copies are relatively scarce;
premium used copies are not.

Caveats
Beware faults and repairs, including
regumming and reperfing. Certificate
recommended for never hinged copies.

3c GREEN
YEAR OF ISSUE: 1879
SCOTT NO. 184

Scarcity
Quantity Issued: 1,335,000,000 est.
★ Average No./Auction: .12

Comments
Refer to the general comments on page 74.
Although this stamp possesses the centering
characteristics of other banknotes, its large
population makes finding premium copies
less difficult. Used copies are abundant.
Never hinged copies exist, and although they
are not common, neither are they scarce.

Premium Characteristics
Refer to the comments on page 74. Premium
unused copies are somewhat less difficult
than higher denominations.

Caveats
Beware faults and repairs, including
regumming and reperfing. Certificate prudent
for never hinged.

5c BLUE
YEAR OF ISSUE: 1879
SCOTT NO. 185

Scarcity
Quantity Issued: 42,000,000 est.
★ Average No./Auction: .44

Comments
Refer to the general comments on page 74.
Never hinged copies are scarce.

Premium Characteristics
Refer to the comments on page 74. Premium
unused copies are difficult.

Caveats
Beware faults and repairs, including
regumming and reperfing. Certificate
recommended for never hinged.

6c PINK
YEAR OF ISSUE: 1879
SCOTT NO. 186

Scarcity
Quantity Issued: 23,650,000 est.
★ Average No./Auction: .43

Comments
Refer to the general comments on page 74.
Color often appears muddy or dingy, and
even at its best is less intense than the other
6-cent banknotes. Nice copies are very
difficult to find. Never hinged copies are
extremely scarce.

Premium Characteristics
Refer to page 74. Both premium unused and
used copies are extremely difficult.

Caveats
Beware faults and repairs, including
regumming and reperfing. Certificate
recommended, essential for never hinged
copies.

10c BROWN, w/o Secret Mark
YEAR OF ISSUE: 1879
SCOTT NO. 187

Scarcity
Quantity Issued: 16,000,000 est.
★ Average No./Auction: .30

Comments
Refer to the general comments on page 74.
Unused copies with balanced margins are
difficult. This stamp is, by far, more scarce
unused than the 15-cent denomination; in
fact, it is much scarcer than most people
realize.

Premium Characteristics
Refer to the comments on page 74. Premium
copies, both unused and used, are difficult.

Caveats
Beware faults and repairs, including
regumming and reperfing. Beware removed
pen cancels. Certificate recommended for
never hinged copies.

10c BROWN, w/ Secret Mark
YEAR OF ISSUE: 1879
SCOTT NO. 188

Scarcity
Quantity Issued: 22,000,000 est.
★ Average No./Auction: .22

Comments
Refer to the general comments on page 74.
Never hinged copies are extremely scarce.
This stamp is, by far, more scarce unused
than the 15-cent denomination.

Premium Characteristics
Refer to the comments on page 74. Premium
copies, both unused and used, are very
difficult.

Caveats
Beware faults and repairs, including
regumming and reperfing. Certificate
recommended, especially for never hinged
copies.

15c RED ORANGE
YEAR OF ISSUE: 1879
SCOTT NO. 189

Scarcity
Quantity Issued: 14,750,000 est.
★ Average No./Auction: .55

Comments
Refer to the general comments on page 74. Never hinged copies are scarce, but not as scarce as the 10-cent values of this series.

Premium Characteristics
Refer to the comments on page 74. Premium copies, although somewhat difficult, are much easier to locate for this value than for nearly any other value of the series.

Caveats
Beware faults and repairs, including regumming and reperfing. Certificate recommended for never hinged copies.

30c BLACK
YEAR OF ISSUE: 1879
SCOTT NO. 190

Scarcity
Quantity Issued: 4,000,000 est.
★ Average No./Auction: .52

Comments
Refer to the general comments on page 74. Never hinged copies are extremely scarce.

Premium Characteristics
Refer to the comments on page 74. Premium copies are very difficult.

Caveats
Beware faults and repairs, including regumming and reperfing. Certificate recommended, essential for never hinged.

90c CARMINE
YEAR OF ISSUE: 1879
SCOTT NO. 191

Scarcity
Quantity Issued: 215,000 est.
★ Average No./Auction: .31
⊚ Average No./Auction: .28

Comments
Refer to the general comments on page 74. This stamp is small margined; copies with balanced margins are difficult. Copies with both balanced margins and nice color are extremely elusive. Never hinged copies are very rare.

Premium Characteristics
Refer to the comments on page 74. Good color. Premium copies, both unused and used, are very difficult.

Caveats
Beware faults and repairs, including regumming and reperfing. Certificate recommended, essential for never hinged copies and copies on cover.

SERIES OF 1879
SPECIAL PRINTING OF 1880
SCOTT NOS. 192-204

Scarcity
Quantity Issued:
For quantities issued, see note under the Special Printing of 1875 on page 72. The 1880 special printing is the much scarcer of the two.

★ Average No./Auction:

No. 192	(1c)	.04
No. 193	(2c)	.07
No. 194	(3c)	.00
No. 195	(6c)	.03
No. 196	(7c)	.06
No. 197	(10c)	.03
No. 198	(12c)	.04
No. 199	(15c)	.04
No. 200	(24c)	.08
No. 201	(30c)	.06
No. 202	(90c)	.03
No. 203	(2c)	.01
No. 204	(5c)	.01

Comments
Issued without gum on soft porous paper. These stamps were valid for postage, however, used copies are generally not known. Because of the very soft paper used for these stamps, thin spots are the rule rather than the exception; they are endemic. Paper inclusions are quite characteristic of this series and not a considered fault. Buyers should be aware of that this stamp is typically poorly centered and be realistic in their expectations; the selection is severely limited. Irregular perfs are not considered a fault. The 2-cent carmine vermilion/scarlet vermilion is much rarer that the figures indicate.

Premium Characteristics
Ideally, copies without faults, however, these stamps are very difficult to locate in any condition. Do not have unreasonably high expectations with respect to quality (especially centering) when considering this issue.

Caveats
Beware faults and repairs. Certificate essential.

Examples of 1880 Special Printing illustrating typical centering for the issue.

5c YELLOW BROWN
YEAR OF ISSUE: 1882
SCOTT NO. 205

Scarcity
Quantity Issued: 167,351,000 est.
★ Average No./Auction: .23

Comments
Refer to the general comments on page 74.
This stamp exists in several shades. Never
hinged copies are scarce.

Premium Characteristics
Refer to comments on page 74. Premium
unused copies are difficult.

Caveats
Beware faults and repairs, including
regumming and reperfing. Certificate
recommended for never hinged.

5c GRAY BROWN
SPECIAL PRINTING OF 1882
SCOTT NO. 205C

Scarcity
Quantity Issued: 2,463
★ Average No./Auction: .00

Comments
Special printing of 1882, issued
without gum on soft porous paper.
Most examples are in relatively nice
condition, and most exist *without*

faults. This stamp is extremely rare, much
rarer than quantity issued would indicate. It
seldom appears on the market. None were
encountered in the auction survey.

Premium Characteristics
This stamp is very difficult to locate in any
condition. Its rarity does not permit selectivity
in the normal sense.

Caveats
Beware faults and repairs. Certificate
essential.

1c GRAY BLUE
YEAR OF ISSUE: 1881
SCOTT NO. 206

Scarcity
Quantity Issued: 3,372,279,000 est.
★ Average No./Auction: .11

Note: Unused, this stamp appears at auction
infrequently because its catalogue value is
relatively low, not because it is scarce.

Comments
Refer to the general comments on page 74.
Exists in several shades. Compared to
previous 1-cent banknotes, it has a much
softer, almost fuzzy appearance. Vivid color,
when encountered, is prized. Never hinged
copies are not common, but neither are they
scarce.

Premium Characteristics
Refer to the comments on page 74. Vivid
color. Premium unused copies are somewhat
difficult, but still much easier than previous 1-
cent banknotes. Premium used copies are
relatively easy because of the stamp's
abundance.

Caveats
Beware faults and repairs, including
regumming and reperfing. Certificate
recommended for never hinged.

3c BLUE GREEN
YEAR OF ISSUE: 1881
SCOTT NO. 207

Scarcity
Quantity Issued: 1,482,380,900
★ Average No./Auction: .12

Note: Appears at auction infrequently unused
because its catalogue value is relatively low.

Comments
Refer to the general comments on page 74.
This stamp's large population makes finding
premium copies only moderately difficult.
Used copies are abundant and premium
copies are easily obtainable. Never hinged
are not common, neither are they scarce.

Premium Characteristics
Refer to the comments on page 74.
Premium unused copies are more difficult that
Scott Nos. 147 and 158. Premium used
copies are not difficult.

Caveats
Beware faults and repairs, including
regumming and reperfing. Certificate
recommended for never hinged.

6c ROSE
YEAR OF ISSUE: 1882
SCOTT NO. 208

Scarcity
Quantity Issued: 11,360,800 est.
★ Average No./Auction: .14

Comments
Refer to the general comments on page 74.
Never hinged copies are very scarce. Comes
in several shades of which the rose shades
are typically muted. Boldly colored examples
are desirable. The brown red shade is more
richly colored, and also very scarce used.

Premium Characteristics
Refer to the comments on page 74. Premium
copies, both unused and used, are difficult.

Caveats
Beware faults and repairs, including
regumming and reperfing. Certificate
recommended for never hinged.

A NOTE ON CONDITION

Nineteenth century stamps are typically poorly centered, lack gum, are heavily canceled, or are
otherwise visually unappealing when compared to modern stamps. Never hinged copies are
quite uncommon and, in some cases, nonexistent. Gum, when present, is often disturbed or
partially missing, the result of heavy paper hinges, which were customary at the time.
Knowledgeable buyers are aware that the condition of gum on early stamps is typically poor and
do not have unrealistic expectations. Faults (including repairs and "improvements" such as
regumming or reperfing) are as common as tumbleweeds on the prairie.
As a general rule, any sound, reasonably centered stamp (within the limitations of the issue),
possessing good color for the issue, and a neat, clear cancel contemporaneous to the issue, if
used, is collectible. The presence of one or more premium characteristics, such as large,
balanced margins, light hinging (or never hinged), fresh, vivid color, is desirable, however, it is
extremely difficult—and sometimes impossible—to find a stamp possessing all the premium
characteristics. Superlative gem copies, when available, command substantial premiums—often
multiples of catalogue.

10c BROWN
YEAR OF ISSUE: 1882
SCOTT NO. 209

Scarcity
Quantity Issued: 146,500,000
★ Average No./Auction: .36

Comments
Refer to the general comments on page 74.
Color is more pronounced than on other
stamps of the 1881-2 issue. The black brown
shade is more difficult to locate, and is
undervalued. Never hinged copies are
relatively scarce.

Premium Characteristics
Refer to page 74. Strong color. Premium
unused copies are somewhat difficult, but still
much easier than the previous series. Premium used copies are not difficult.

Caveats
Beware faults and repairs, including
regumming and reperfing. Certificate
recommended for never hinged.

2c RED BROWN
YEAR OF ISSUE: 1883
SCOTT NO. 210

Scarcity
Quantity Issued: 4,320,000,000 est.
★ Average No./Auction: .32 *

Comments
Refer to the general comments on page 74.
Never hinged copies are not common, but
neither are they scarce.

Premium Characteristics
Refer to the comments on page 74. Premium
unused copies are not difficult. Used stamps
are extremely common.

Caveats
Beware faults and repairs, including
regumming and reperfing. Certificate
recommended for never hinged.

* Note: Appears at auction infrequently unused because
its catalogue value is relatively low.

4c BLUE GREEN
YEAR OF ISSUE: 1883
SCOTT NO. 211

Scarcity
Quantity Issued: 78,500,000
★ Average No./Auction: .26

Comments
Refer to the general comments on page 74.
Copies with deep, intense color are prized.
Never hinged copies are scarce.

Premium Characteristics
Refer to the comments on page 74. Strong
color. Premium unused copies are difficult.

Caveats
Beware faults and repairs, including
regumming and reperfing. Certificate
recommended for never hinged.

Comments
Refer to the general comments on page 74.
Issued with gum on soft porous paper.
Never hinged copies are very scarce. Used
copies are exceedingly rare.

Premium Characteristics
Refer to the comments on page 74. Premium
copies are difficult.

2c PALE RED BROWN
SPECIAL PRINTING OF 1883
SCOTT NO. 211B

Caveats
Beware faults and repairs. Certificate
essential.

Scarcity
Quantity Issued: less than 200 est.
★ Average No./Auction: .40

4c DEEP BLUE GREEN
SPECIAL PRINTING OF 1883
SCOTT NO. 211D

Scarcity
Quantity Issued: 26
★ Average No./Auction: .01

Comments
This stamp is extremely rare. Issued
without gum on soft porous paper.
Like Scott No. 205C, most known

examples are of fairly nice quality. Used
copies are generally unknown.

Premium Characteristics
This stamp is difficult to locate in any
condition. Its rarity does not permit selectivity
in the normal sense.

Caveats
Certificate essential.

Comments
Refer to the general comments on page 74.
Color often appears faded or washed out.
Never hinged copies are not common, but
neither are they scarce.

Premium Characteristics
Refer to the comments on page 74. Premium
unused copies are difficult. Used copies are
abundant; premium copies are easily
obtainable.

1c ULTRAMARINE
YEAR OF ISSUE: 1887
SCOTT NO. 212

Caveats
Beware faults and repairs, including
regumming and reperfing. Certificate
recommended for never hinged.

Scarcity
Quantity Issued: 1,325,000,000 est.
★ Average No./Auction: .18 *

* Note: Appears at auction infrequently unused because
its catalogue value is relatively low.

2c GREEN
YEAR OF ISSUE: 1887
SCOTT NO. 213

Scarcity
Quantity Issued: 3,580,000,000 est.
★ Average No./Auction: .24 *

Comments
Refer to the general comments on page 74.
Never hinged copies are not common, but
neither are they scarce.

Premium Characteristics
Refer to the comments on page 74. Premium
unused copies are not difficult. Used copies
are abundant; premium copies are easily
obtainable.

Caveats
Certificate recommended for never hinged.

* Note: Appears at auction infrequently unused because
its catalogue value is relatively low.

3c VERMILION
YEAR OF ISSUE: 1887
SCOTT NO. 214

Scarcity
Quantity Issued: 15,000,000 est.
★ Average No./Auction: .35 *

Comments
Refer to the general comments on page 74.
Never hinged copies are not common, but
neither are they scarce.

Premium Characteristics
Refer to the comments on page 74. Vivid
color. Premium unused copies are only
moderately difficult.

Caveats
Beware faults and repairs, including
regumming and reperfing. Certificate
recommended for never hinged.

* Note: Appears at auction infrequently unused because
its catalogue value is relatively low.

4c CARMINE
YEAR OF ISSUE: 1888
SCOTT NO. 215

Scarcity
Quantity Issued: 24,500,000 est.
★ Average No./Auction: .46

Comments
Refer to the general comments on page 74.
Color is susceptible to chemical discoloration.
Bright, fresh copies are the most desirable.
Never hinged copies are relatively scarce.

Premium Characteristics
Refer to the comments on page 74. Premium
unused copies are difficult; premium used
copies are surprisingly difficult.

Caveats
Beware faults and repairs, including
regumming and reperfing. Certificate
recommended for never hinged.

5c INDIGO
YEAR OF ISSUE: 1888
SCOTT NO. 216

Scarcity
Quantity Issued: 85,000,000 est.
★ Average No./Auction: .27

Comments
Refer to the general comments on page 74.
Never hinged copies are not common.

Premium Characteristics
Refer to the comments on page 74. Premium
unused copies are difficult.

Caveats
Beware faults and repairs, including
regumming and reperfing. Certificate
recommended for never hinged.

30c ORANGE BROWN
YEAR OF ISSUE: 1888
SCOTT NO. 217

Scarcity
Quantity Issued: 915,000 est.
★ Average No./Auction: .74

Comments
Refer to the general comments on page 74.
One of the easiest banknotes to find well
centered and nicely margined. Never hinged
copies are very scarce.

Premium Characteristics
Refer to the comments on page 74. Never
hinged is the most difficult of the premium
characteristics. Copies possessing all the
premium qualities are difficult.

Caveats
Beware faults and repairs, including
regumming and reperfing. Certificate
recommended for never hinged copies and
essential for used stamp on cover.

90c PURPLE
YEAR OF ISSUE: 1888
SCOTT NO. 218

Scarcity
Quantity Issued: 135,000
★ Average No./Auction: .59
⊙ Average No./Auction: .62

Comments
Refer to the general comments on page 74.
Never hinged copies are very scarce.

Premium Characteristics
Refer to the comments on page 74. Good
color. Premium copies are extremely difficult.

Caveats
Beware faults and repairs, including
regumming and reperfing. Certificate
recommended for never hinged copies and
essential for stamp on cover.

SERIES OF 1890-93
GENERAL COMMENTS
SCOTT NOS. 219-29

Scarcity
Quantities Issued:

No. 219	(1c)	2,206,093,450	
No. 219D	(2c lake)	100,000,000	est.
No. 220	(2c)	6,244,719,500	est.
No. 221	(3c)	46,877,250	
No. 222	(4c)	66,759,475	
No. 223	(5c)	152,236,530	
No. 224	(6c)	9,253,400	
No. 225	(8c)	12,087,800	
No. 226	(10c)	70,591,710	
No. 227	(15c)	5,548,710	
No. 228	(30c)	1,735,018	
No. 229	(90c)	219,721	

General Comments
Stamps of this series are typically poorly centered. The 1- and 2-cent values are abundant used, so premium copies are easy to find. Used copies of the other values, while not scarce, are typically heavily canceled. Attractive copies are difficult to locate.

Unused copies suffer from all the problems that afflict nineteenth century stamps: heavy hinging, disturbed gum, poor centering, small margins, and faults. Irregular perfs are frequently encountered—but not as often as on the earlier hard-paper nineteenth century issues—and are not considered a fault. Premium copies are surprisingly difficult. The lower values are easier to locate never hinged because most never hinged stock comes from blocks, and fewer blocks of high values were saved. From the survey, it appears that about 20 percent of the high values (15-90-cent) appearing at auction were never hinged.

ONE CENT. Exists in a variety of shades, some of which are dull and unattractive. Bright shades are more visually appealing and desirable.
TWO CENT. The lake shade (No. 219D) is difficult in premium condition and very scarce never hinged.
THREE CENT. Often weakly colored. Strong shades are the most desirable.
FOUR CENT. Very scarce in premium condition.
SIX CENT. Often appears washed out, especially used. Strong shades are the most desirable. Very scarce in premium condition.
EIGHT CENT. Often appears washed out, especially used. Strongly colored examples are the most desirable.
TEN CENT. Very scarce in premium condition.

Premium Characteristics
Sound condition, balanced margins (jumbo margined copies are prized and worth a substantial premium), fresh color, lightly hinged or never hinged, if unused; neat, clear cancel, if used. Premium unused copies are difficult, especially the 4-cent, 6-cent, and 10-cent values.

Caveats
Beware faults and repairs, including regumming and reperfing. Certificate recommended for never hinged on the more expensive stamps of the series.

Examples of gem quality 1890-1893 stamps.

1890-93 SERIES HIGH VALUES

15c INDIGO
SCOTT NO. 227

Scarcity
Quantity Issued: 5,548,710
★ Average No./Auction: .32

Comments
Refer to the general comments on page 85.
Never hinged copies are scarce. Rich, vividly
color examples are prized.

Premium Characteristics
Refer to the comments on page 85. Vivid
color. Premium copies are difficult.

Caveats
Beware faults and repairs, including
regumming and reperfing. Certificate
recommended for never hinged.

30c BLACK
SCOTT NO. 228

Scarcity
Quantity Issued: 1,735,018
★ Average No./Auction: .48

Comments
Refer to the general comments on page 85.
Never hinged copies are scarce. Intensely
colored copies are prized.

Premium Characteristics
Refer to the comments on page 85. Vivid
color. Premium copies are difficult.

Caveats
Beware faults and repairs, including
regumming and reperfing. Certificate
recommended for never hinged.

90c ORANGE
SCOTT NO. 229

Scarcity
Quantity Issued: 219,721
★ Average No./Auction: .62

Comments
Refer to the general comments on page 85.
Never hinged copies are scarce. Several
shades exist. Color is often poor. Intensely
colored copies are prized.

Premium Characteristics
Refer to the comments on page 85. Vivid
color. Premium copies are difficult.

Caveats
Beware faults and repairs, including
regumming and reperfing. Certificate
recommended for never hinged.

COLUMBIAN SERIES OF 1893
GENERAL COMMENTS
SCOTT NOS. 230-45

Scarcity
Quantities Issued:

No. 230	(1c)	449,195,550
No. 231	(2c)	1,464,588,750
No. 232	(3c)	11,501,250
No. 233	(4c)	19,181,550
No. 234	(5c)	35,248,250
No. 235	(6c)	4,707,550
No. 236	(8c)	10,656,550
No. 237	(10c)	16,516,950
No. 238	(15c)	1,576,950
No. 239	(30c)	617,250
No. 240	(50c)	243,750
No. 241	($1)	55,050
No. 242	($2)	45,550
No. 243	($3)	27,650
No. 244	($4)	26,350
No. 245	($5)	27,350

General Comments
Margins on this series tend to be larger than on definitive stamps of the same era. The 1- and 2-cent values are abundant used, so premium copies are easy to find. Used copies of the other values up to the $1, while not scarce, are typically heavily canceled, poorly centered, or faulty. Nevertheless, because the issue was so popular, large populations of used stamps exist for values up to the dollar denominations; low values are not terribly difficult to find in premium condition.

Finding premium copies of unused Columbians, even the lower values, is much more difficult. Unused copies are often heavily hinged or exhibit disturbed gum.

This series was widely saved, often in blocks, which are the source of today's never hinged copies. As a consequence, never hinged Columbians are more plentiful (except the dollar values) than definitives of the era.

In order to improve the appearance of heavily hinged copies, many have been regummed. Regumming is especially a problem on high values; buyers should be cautious of examples offered as never hinged. Reperfing is also commonplace, as are other kinds of tampering. Scrutinize stamps very carefully for signs of tampering.

Unused dollar values are plagued by the poor centering, faults, toned paper, regumming, and reperfing. Premium copies of dollar values are surprisingly difficult. Individual dollar values are covered in more detail immediately following this section.

The 4-cent often looks dingy, especially when its paper is toned.
The 6-cent is susceptible to fading.
The 8-cent often appears dingy.
The 10-cent is often faulty and poorly centered.
The 30-cent is susceptible to chemical color change. Bright color is prized.

Premium Characteristics
Sound condition, balanced margins (jumbo margined copies are prized and worth a substantial premium), fresh color, lightly hinged or never hinged, if unused; neat, clear (non-obliterative) cancel of the period, if used. Unused premium copies of the dollar values are exceedingly difficult.

Caveats
Beware faults and repairs, including regumming, reperfing, and tampering, even on the lower values. Certificate recommended for higher values in general, and is essential for never hinged higher values.

Note: At least three "original gums" are found on the Columbians: 1. white crackly gum with many gum creases and paper cracks; 2. pale yellowish gum; 3. striated brownish gum, which is thick and tough.

50c SLATE BLUE
YEAR OF ISSUE: 1893
SCOTT NO. 240

Scarcity
Quantity Issued: 243,750
★ Average No./Auction: 1.41
⊘ Average No./Auction: .31

Hinging
NH: 11.4%
Hinged: 88.6%

Comments
Refer to the general comments on page 87.
Regumming and reperfing are commonplace.
Never hinged copies are very scarce.

Premium Characteristics
Refer to the comments on page 87. Deep
shades are prized. Premium unused copies
are difficult; premium used copies are
surprisingly difficult. The illustrated example
is a gem.

Caveats
Beware faults and repairs, especially
regumming and reperfing. Certificate
recommended for never hinged.

$1 SALMON
YEAR OF ISSUE: 1893
SCOTT NO. 241

Scarcity
Quantity Issued: 55,050
★ Average No./Auction: 2.21
⊘ Average No./Auction: .67

Hinging
NH: 5.4%
Hinged: 94.6%

Comments
Refer to the general comments on page 87.
This stamp is somewhat smaller margined
than other high value Columbians. Faults are
quite commonplace. The color often appears
weak, especially on used copies, and is
susceptible to chemical change. Used copies
are typically heavily cancelled. Regumming
and reperfing are frequently encountered.
Never hinged copies are very rare.

Premium Characteristics
Refer to the comments on page 87.
Pronounced color is prized. Premium copies,
unused or used, are extremely difficult. This
stamp is generally regarded as the most
difficult of the dollar value Columbians to find
in premium quality. The illustrated example is
a gem.

Caveats
Beware faults and repairs, especially
regumming and reperfing. Certificate
recommended for unused and used, and is
essential for never hinged.

Refer to page 91 for additional illustrations.

$2 BROWN RED
YEAR OF ISSUE: 1893
SCOTT NO. 242

Scarcity
Quantity Issued: 45,550
★ Average No./Auction: 2.07
๏ Average No./Auction: .88

Hinging
NH: 5.4%
Hinged: 94.6%

Comments
Refer to the general comments on page 87.
Color can appear washed out, especially on
used copies, and may be susceptible to light.
Used copies are usually heavily cancelled.
Faults are quite commonplace. Gum is
typically heavily hinged or disturbed.
Regumming and reperfing are frequently
encountered. Never hinged copies are very
rare.

Premium Characteristics
Refer to the comments on page 87. Fresh
color. Premium unused copies are extremely
difficult; premium used copies are difficult.
The illustrated example is a gem.

Caveats
Beware faults and repairs, especially
regumming and reperfing. Certificate
recommended for unused and used, and is
essential for never hinged.

$3 YELLOW GREEN
YEAR OF ISSUE: 1893
SCOTT NO. 243

Scarcity
Quantity Issued: 27,650
★ Average No./Auction: 1.92
๏ Average No./Auction: .42

Hinging
NH: 3.2%
Hinged: 96.8%

Comments
Refer to the general comments on page 87.
Faults are irritatingly commonplace. Color
often appears washed out, especially on used
copies, and may be fugitive. Bright, vividly
colored copies are prized. The olive green
shade is desirable and worth a premium.
Used copies are usually heavily cancelled.
Gum is typically heavily hinged or disturbed.
Regumming and reperfing are frequently
encountered. Never hinged copies are very
rare.

Premium Characteristics
Refer to the comments on page 87. Strong
color. Premium copies, unused or used, are
extremely difficult. The illustrated example is
a gem.

Caveats
Beware faults and repairs, especially
regumming and reperfing. Certificate
recommended for unused and used, and is
essential for never hinged.

Refer to page 91 for additional illustrations.

$4 CRIMSON LAKE
YEAR OF ISSUE: 1893
SCOTT NO. 244

Scarcity
Quantity Issued: 26,350
★ Average No./Auction: 2.17
⊙ Average No./Auction: .60

Hinging
NH: 2.3%
Hinged: 97.7%

Comments
Refer to the general comments on page 87. Faults are annoyingly commonplace. Color is fugitive and often appears washed out, especially on used copies. Bright, vividly colored copies are scarce and highly prized. Used copies are usually heavily cancelled. Gum is typically hinged or disturbed. Regumming and reperfing are frequently encountered. Never hinged copies are extremely rare.

Premium Characteristics
Refer to the comments on page 87. Vivid color. Premium unused copies are exceedingly difficult; premium used copies are very difficult. The illustrated example is a gem.

Caveats
Beware faults and repairs, especially regumming and reperfing. Certificate recommended for unused and used, and is essential for never hinged.

$5 BLACK
YEAR OF ISSUE: 1893
SCOTT NO. 245

Scarcity
Quantity Issued: 27,350
★ Average No./Auction: 2.03
⊙ Average No./Auction: .59

Hinging
NH: 0.5%
Hinged: 99.5%

Comments
Refer to the general comments on page 87. Faults are commonplace; in fact, the vast majority of this value have small imperfections. Used copies are usually heavily cancelled. Gum is typically heavily hinged or disturbed. Regumming and reperfing are frequently encountered. Never hinged copies are very exceedingly rare.

Premium Characteristics
Refer to the comments on page 87. Fresh color. Premium copies, unused or used, are exceedingly difficult. The illustrated example is a gem.

Caveats
Beware faults and repairs, especially regumming and reperfing. Certificate essential for never hinged.

1893 COLUMBIAN SERIES
CENTERING & CANCELLATIONS

Centering on the Columbians is quite variable as the photos of typical copies below illustrate. Cancellations tend to be heavy.

$1 Salmon

$2 Brown Red

$3 Yellow Green

$4 Crimson Lake

$5 Black

SERIES OF 1894
GENERAL COMMENTS
SCOTT NOS. 246-63

Scarcity
Quantity Issued:

No. 246	(1c ultra)	100,000,000 est.
No. 247	(1c blue)	305,000,000 est.
No. 248	(2c pink)	40,000,000 est.
No. 249	(2c c. lake)	100,000,000 est.
No. 250	(2c carm.)	910,000,000 est.
No. 251	(2c, Ty II)	100,000,000 est.
No. 252	(2c, Ty III)	80,000,000 est.
No. 253	(3c)	20,214,300
No. 254	(4c)	16,718,150
No. 255	(5c)	30,688,840
No. 256	(6c)	5,120,800
No. 257	(8c)	2,426,100
No. 258	(10c)	12,263,180
No. 259	(15c)	1,583,920
No. 260	(50c)	175,330
No. 261	($1, Ty I)	26,284
No. 261A	($1, Ty II)	8,762
No. 262	($2)	10,027
No. 263	($5)	6,251

General Comments
Stamps of this series are typically small margined and poorly centered. Gum is usually heavily hinged or disturbed. Most never hinged stock comes from blocks, therefore, never hinged low values are more plentiful than high values. Faults are commonplace.

The paper used to print this series is generally poor. Irregular, rough, or incompletely punched perfs are frequently encountered and not considered a fault. Too-clean, razor-sharp holes may indicate reperfing.

The 1- and 2-cent values are abundant used, so premium copies are easy to find. Used copies of the other values, while not scarce, are notorious for being heavily canceled. Attractive copies are the exception, and surprisingly difficult.

The 1-cent blue (No. 247) often appears pale and washed out. Brightly colored copies are the most desirable. The same holds true for the 2-cent pink (No. 248). Unused copies of the more expensive 2-cent varieties contain irritating flaws, are surprisingly difficult in premium condition, and scarce never hinged.

The 3-cent often is weakly colored. Strong shades are prized.

The 5-cent exists in a variety of shades.

The 6-cent is probably the most difficult of the lower values to locate in premium condition. Color is often poor, especially used. Vividly colored copies are prized.

The 8-cent is susceptible to fading. Richly colored copies are prized. This stamp is moderately priced unused, but difficult to locate in premium condition.

The 10- and 15-cent values are afflicted by poor centering, heavy cancels, heavy hinging or disturbed gum.

The higher values are analyzed separately following these general comments.

Premium Characteristics
Sound condition, balanced margins (jumbo margined copies are worth a substantial premium), fresh color, lightly hinged or never hinged, if unused; neat, non-obliterative cancel, if used. Premium copies above the 3-cent are scarce, unused or used. Premium copies of the high values are rare.

Caveats
Beware faults and repairs, including regumming and reperfing. Certificate recommended for never hinged, especially the more expensive stamps of the series.

Note: Two types of original gum exist for this series: 1. Thin, white, very crackly gum prone to gum creasing and paper cracking; 2. Even, yellowish, thicker gum, which gives a deeper color but does not cause gum creasing and paper cracking.

Series of 1894. Examples of centering at left, including typical heavy cancel at bottom. The enlarged stamps on the right are incredible large-margined gems.

50c ORANGE
YEAR OF ISSUE: 1894
SCOTT NO. 260

Scarcity
Quantity Issued: 175,330
★ Average No./Auction: .65

Hinging
NH: 4.7%
Hinged: 95.3%

Comments
Refer to the general comments on page 92. Color is often weak. Fresh, brightly colored copies are very scarce and highly prized. Used copies are usually heavily cancelled. Regumming and reperfing are common.

Premium Characteristics
Sound condition, balanced margins, bright color, lightly hinged or never hinged original gum, if unused; neat, non-obliterative cancel, if used. Premium copies are difficult. The illustrated example is a gem.

Caveats
Beware faults and repairs, including regumming and reperfing. Certificate strongly recommended for never hinged.

$1 BLACK, Type I
YEAR OF ISSUE: 1894
SCOTT NO. 261

Scarcity
Quantity Issued: 26,284
★ Average No./Auction: .64
⊙ Average No./Auction: .11

Hinging
NH: 7.9%
Hinged: 92.1%

Comments
Refer to the general comments on page 92. Used copies are usually heavily cancelled. Never hinged copies are very rare. Although issued in numbers comparable to the high value Columbians, this stamp is much more difficult to locate in decent condition.

Premium Characteristics
Sound condition, balanced margins, strong color, lightly hinged or never hinged original gum, if unused; neat, non-obliterative cancel, if used. Premium copies, both unused and used, are exceedingly difficult.

Caveats
Beware faults and repairs, including regumming and reperfing. Certificate essential for never hinged.

$1 BLACK, Type II
YEAR OF ISSUE: 1894
SCOTT NO. 261A

Scarcity
Quantity Issued: 8,762
★ Average No./Auction: .47
⊙ Average No./Auction: .12

Hinging
NH: 4.3%
Hinged: 95.7%

Comments
Refer to the general comments on page 92. A very scarce stamp, whose small population makes it exceedingly difficult to locate in premium condition either unused or used. Used copies are usually heavily cancelled, and extremely difficult in decent condition. Very rare never hinged.

Premium Characteristics
Sound condition, balanced margins, fresh color, lightly hinged or never hinged original gum, if unused; neat, non-obliterative cancel, if used. Premium copies, unused or used, are exceedingly rare. The illustrated example is a gem.

Caveats
Beware faults and repairs, including regumming and reperfing. Certificate recommended for unused, and essential for never hinged.

$2 BRIGHT BLUE
YEAR OF ISSUE: 1894
SCOTT NO. 262

Scarcity
Quantity Issued: 10,027
★ Average No./Auction: .65
⊘ Average No./Auction: .13

Hinging
NH: 3.2%
Hinged: 96.8%

Comments
Refer to the general comments on page 92. A very scarce stamp, whose small population makes it exceedingly difficult to locate to premium condition either unused or used. Used copies are usually heavily cancelled. Never hinged copies are very rare.

Premium Characteristics
Sound condition, balanced margins, strong color, lightly hinged or never hinged original gum, if unused; neat, non-obliterative cancel, if used. Premium copies, both unused and used, are exceedingly difficult. The illustrated example is a gem.

Caveats
Beware faults and repairs, including regumming and reperfing. Certificate recommended for all copies and essential for never hinged.

$5 DARK GREEN
YEAR OF ISSUE: 1894
SCOTT NO. 263

Scarcity
Quantity Issued: 6,251
★ Average No./Auction: .65
⊘ Average No./Auction: .11

Hinging
NH: 0.0%
Hinged: 100.0%

Comments
Refer to the general comments on page 92. A very rare stamp, whose small population makes it exceedingly difficult to locate in premium condition either unused or used. Used copies are usually heavily cancelled. It is exceedingly rare never hinged; in fact, none were encountered in the auction survey.

Premium Characteristics
Sound condition, balanced margins, fresh color, lightly hinged, original gum, if unused; neat, non-obliterative cancel, if used. Premium copies, both unused and used, are exceedingly rare. The illustrated example is a gem.

Caveats
Beware faults and repairs, including regumming and reperfing. Certificate recommended for all copies and essential for never hinged.

SERIES OF 1895
Double Line Watermark
GENERAL COMMENTS
SCOTT NOS. 264-78

Scarcity
Quantity Issued:

No. 264	(1c blue)	1,971,338,663	est.
No. 265	(2c Ty I)	300,000,000	est.
No. 266	(2c Ty II)	125,000,000	est.
No. 267	(2c Ty III)	7,475,000,000	est.
No. 268	(3c)	203,057,170	
No. 269	(4c)	78,167,836	est.
No. 270	(5c)	123,775,455	est.
No. 271	(6c)	20,712,875	est.
No. 272	(8c)	96,217,820	
No. 273	(10c)	59,983,007	est.
No. 274	(15c)	7,013,612	
No. 275	(50c)	1,065,390	
No. 276	($1 Ty I)	192,449	
No. 276A	($1 Ty II)	63,803	
No. 277	($2)	31,720	
No. 278	($5)	26,965	

General Comments
Stamps of this series are typically small margined and poorly centered. Gum is usually heavily hinged or disturbed. Faults are commonplace.

Used copies are notorious for heavy cancels, however, the lower values are sufficiently abundant to make locating premium copies fairly easy.

Most never hinged stock comes from blocks, therefore, the low values are easier to locate never hinged than the high values. Premium unused copies of this series are less difficult to find than those of the 1894 Series. Knowledgeable buyers look for fresh, boldly colored examples and avoid those on toned paper.

ONE CENT (No. 264). Occurs in a variety of shades, the deeply colored ones being most appealing. Not difficult in premium condition unused or used.

TWO CENT, Type I (No. 265). Not difficult to locate in premium condition either unused or used.

TWO CENT, Type II (No. 266). Somewhat difficult to locate in premium condition unused.

TWO CENT, Type III (No. 267). Not difficult to locate in premium condition either unused or used.

THREE CENT (No. 268). Color sometimes weak, washed out. Not difficult to locate in premium condition either unused or used.

FOUR CENT (No. 269). Crisply colored copies are prized. Plate wear gives later copies a fuzzy, indistinct appearance. Not difficult to locate in premium condition either unused or used.

FIVE CENT (No. 270). Color varies and can be poor. Not difficult to locate in premium condition either unused or used.

SIX CENT (No. 271). Color often poor. Crisply colored copies are prized. More difficult to locate in premium condition both unused or used.

EIGHT CENT (No. 272). Crisply colored copies are prized. More difficult to locate in premium condition both unused or used.

TEN CENT (No. 273). One of the least difficult of the series in premium condition, however, unused copies are somewhat scarce.

FIFTEEN CENT (No. 274). Difficult to locate in premium condition unused.

Premium Characteristics
Sound condition, balanced margins (jumbo margined copies are prized and worth a substantial premium), fresh color, lightly hinged or never hinged, if unused; neat, non-obliterative cancel, if used.

Caveats
Beware faults and repairs, including regumming and reperfing. Certificate recommended for never hinged, especially on the more expensive stamps of the series.

Note: The designs for this 1895 series are identical to those of the 1894 series. The series differs only in that it was printed on watermarked paper.

Expect to pay a premium for uncharacteristically superlative centering such as above.

50c ORANGE
Double Line Watermark
YEAR OF ISSUE: 1895
SCOTT NO. 275

Scarcity
Quantity Issued: 1,065,390
★ Average No./Auction: .44

Hinging
NH: 9.1%
Hinged: 90.9%

Comments
Refer to the general comments on page 96. Color is often poor. Fresh, brightly colored copies are very scarce and highly prized. Regumming and reperfing are commonplace. Never hinged copies are scarce.

Premium Characteristics
Sound condition, balanced margins, bright color, lightly hinged or never hinged original gum, if unused; neat, non-obliterative cancel, if used. Premium unused copies are difficult; premium used copies, although not expensive, are difficult.

Caveats
Beware faults and repairs, including regumming and reperfing. Certificate strongly recommended for never hinged.

$1 BLACK, Type I
Double Line Watermark
YEAR OF ISSUE: 1895
SCOTT NO. 276

Scarcity
Quantity Issued: 192,449
★ Average No./Auction: .79
⊚ Average No./Auction: .15

Hinging
NH: 9.1%
Hinged: 90.9%

Comments
Refer to the general comments on page 96. Regumming and reperfing are commonplace. Never hinged copies are very scarce.

Premium Characteristics
Sound condition, balanced margins, fresh color, lightly hinged or never hinged original gum, if unused; neat, non-obliterative cancel, if used. Premium copies are very difficult.

Caveats
Beware faults and repairs, including regumming and reperfing. Certificate recommended; essential for never hinged copies and those on cover.

$1 BLACK, Type II
Double Line Watermark
YEAR OF ISSUE: 1895
SCOTT NO. 276A

Scarcity
Quantity Issued: 63,803
★ Average No./Auction: .42
๏ Average No./Auction: .12

Hinging
NH: 0.0%
Hinged: 100.0%

Comments
Refer to the general comments on page 96. A very scarce stamp whose small population makes it exceedingly difficult to locate in premium condition either unused or used. Never hinged copies are very rare; in fact, none were encountered in the auction survey.

Premium Characteristics
Sound condition, balanced margins, fresh color, lightly hinged or never hinged original gum, if unused; neat, non-obliterative cancel, if used. Premium copies are very rare.

Caveats
Beware faults and repairs, including regumming and reperfing. Certificate recommended; essential for never hinged copies and for those on cover.

$2 BRIGHT BLUE
Double Line Watermark
YEAR OF ISSUE: 1895
SCOTT NO. 277

Scarcity
Quantity Issued: 31,720
★ Average No./Auction: .77
๏ Average No./Auction: .23

Hinging
NH: 0.0%
Hinged: 100.0%

Comments
Refer to the general comments on page 96. A very scarce stamp whose small population makes it exceedingly difficult to locate in premium condition either unused or used. Never hinged copies are very rare; in fact, none were encountered in the auction survey.

Premium Characteristics
Sound condition, balanced margins, strong color, lightly hinged or never hinged original gum, if unused; neat, non-obliterative cancel, if used. Premium copies are exceedingly difficult.

Caveats
Beware faults and repairs, including regumming and reperfing. Certificate recommended; essential for never hinged copies and those on cover.

$5 DARK GREEN
Double Line Watermark
YEAR OF ISSUE: 1895
SCOTT NO. 278

Scarcity
Quantity Issued: 26,965
★ Average No./Auction: .94
๏ Average No./Auction: .66

Hinging
NH: 5.4%
Hinged: 94.6%

Comments
Refer to the general comments on page 96. A very scarce stamp whose small population makes it exceedingly difficult to locate in premium condition either unused or used. It is very rare never hinged.

Premium Characteristics
Sound condition, balanced margins, fresh color, lightly hinged or never hinged original gum, if unused; neat, non-obliterative cancel, if used. Premium copies are very rare.

Caveats
Beware faults and repairs, including regumming and reperfing. Certificate recommended; essential for never hinged copies and those on cover.

SERIES OF 1898
Double Line Watermark
Same Designs as Previous Issue,
New Colors
GENERAL COMMENTS
SCOTT NOS. 279-84

Scarcity
Quantity Issued:

No. 279	(1c)	5,216,159,932	est.
No. 279B	(2c T II)	12,000,000,000	est.
No. 280	(4c)	153,499,379	est.
No. 281	(5c)	279,622,170	est.
No. 282	(6c)	46,457,540	est.
No. 282C	(10c Ty I)	42,000,000	est.
No. 283	(10c Ty II)	65,000,000	est.
No. 284	(15c)	51,993,313	

General Comments
Stamps of this series are typically small margined and poorly centered. Gum is usually heavily hinged or disturbed. Faults are commonplace. Irregular perfs are frequently encountered and not considered a fault.

Although used copies are notorious for heavy cancels, they are sufficiently abundant to make locating premium copies fairly easy.

Most never hinged stock comes from blocks, therefore, the NH low values are easier to locate than high values.

In general, premium unused copies are less difficult to locate than those of the 1894 or 1895 Series. Knowledgeable buyers look for fresh, boldly colored examples and avoid those on toned paper.

ONE CENT (No. 279). Not difficult in premium condition either unused or used.
TWO CENT, Type III (No. 279B). Not difficult in premium condition either unused or used.
FOUR CENT (No. 280). Comes in many shades. Crisply colored copies are prized. Premium unused copies are moderately difficult.
FIVE CENT (No. 281). Premium unused copies are moderately difficult.
SIX CENT (No. 282). Comes in many shades. Crisply colored copies are prized. Premium unused copies are moderately difficult.
TEN CENT, Type I (No. 282C). The most difficult of the series. Centering always a problem. Premium unused copies are moderately difficult.
TEN CENT, Type II (No. 283). Centering always a problem. Premium unused copies are moderately difficult.
FIFTEEN CENT (No. 284). Many interesting shade varieties exist. Premium unused copies are moderately difficult.

Premium Characteristics
Sound condition, balanced margins (jumbo margined copies are prized and worth a substantial premium), fresh color, lightly hinged or never hinged, if unused; neat, non-obliterative cancel, if used.

Caveats
Beware faults and repairs, including regumming and reperfing. Certificate recommended for never hinged, especially on the more expensive stamps of the series.

TRANS-MISSISSIPPI SERIES OF 1898
GENERAL COMMENTS
SCOTT NOS. 285-93

Scarcity
Quantity Issued:

No. 285	(1c)	70,993,400
No. 286	(2c)	159,720,800
No. 287	(4c)	4,924,500
No. 288	(5c)	7,694,180
No. 289	(8c)	2,927,200
No. 290	(10c)	4,629,760
No. 291	(50c)	530,400
No. 292	($1)	56,900
No. 293	($2)	46,200

General Comments
Margins on this series tend to be larger than on definitive stamps of the same era. Gum is often heavily hinged or disturbed. Irregular perfs are frequently encountered and not considered a fault. The 1- and 2-cent values are abundant used; premium copies are easy to find. Used copies of the other values up to the $1, while not scarce, are typically heavily canceled, poorly centered, or faulty. However, a large population of used stamps exists for values up to the 50-cent denomination. With diligence, premium used copies of these values are only moderately difficult to locate. Premium unused Trans-Mississippis, even the lower values, are much more difficult. Collectors saved a fair number of blocks, which are the source of today's never hinged copies. Never hinged Trans-Mississippis are more plentiful (except dollar values) than definitives of the era. In order to improve the appearance of heavily hinged copies, many have been regummed. Regumming is especially a problem on high values; buyers should be cautious of copies offered as never hinged. Reperfing is also commonplace on the dollar values, as are other forms of tampering such as filled thins, etc. Unused dollar values are plagued by the poor centering, faults, toned paper, regumming, or reperfing, and premium copies are surprisingly difficult. Individual dollar values are covered in more detail on pages following this section.

ONE CENT (No. 285). Premium unused copies are somewhat difficult.
TWO CENT (No. 286). Premium copies, unused or used, are not difficult.
FOUR CENT (No. 287). Color susceptible to chemical change (browning). Crisply colored copies more desirable. Premium unused copies are moderately difficult.
FIVE CENT (No. 288). Premium unused copies are moderately difficult.
EIGHT CENT (No. 289). This value, along with the $2, is the smallest margined of the series, and surprisingly difficult to locate unused in premium condition. Large margined copies are rare.
TEN CENT (No. 290). Large margined copies much easier to locate than the 8-cent value. Premium unused copies are difficult.

Premium Characteristics
Sound condition, balanced margins (jumbo margined copies are prized and worth a substantial premium), fresh color, lightly hinged or never hinged, if unused; neat, non-obliterative cancel, if used.

Caveats
Beware faults and repairs, including regumming, reperfing, and tampering, even on the lower values. Certificate recommended for all high values in general, and is essential for never hinged high values.

50c Sage Green

$1 Black

$2 Orange Brown (Note the typical small margins on this value.)

50c SAGE GREEN
YEAR OF ISSUE: 1898
SCOTT NO. 291

Scarcity
Quantity Issued: 530,400
★ Average No./Auction: 1.69
⊙ Average No./Auction: .42

Hinging
NH: 9.0%
Hinged: 91.0%

Comments
This stamp is typically poorly centered. Nicely centered copies are very scarce. Used copies are usually heavily canceled. Faults are commonplace. Gum is typically heavily hinged or disturbed. Never hinged copies are very scarce.

Premium Characteristics
Sound condition, balanced margins, fresh color, lightly hinged or never hinged original gum, if unused; neat, non-obliterative cancel, if used. Premium copies are very difficult.

Caveats
Beware faults and repairs, including regumming and reperfing. Certificate recommended in general; essential for never hinged copies and those on cover.

$1 BLACK
YEAR OF ISSUE: 1898
SCOTT NO. 292

Scarcity
Quantity Issued: 56,900
★ Average No./Auction: 2.84
⊚ Average No./Auction: 1.07

Hinging
NH: 9.3%
Hinged: 90.7%

Comments
A very scarce stamp, whose small population makes it exceedingly

difficult to locate in premium condition either unused or used. This stamp is typically poorly centered, however, a substantial number of well-centered copies do exist. Faults are commonplace. Regumming and reperfing are frequently encountered. Used copies are usually heavily cancelled. Gum is typically heavily hinged or disturbed. Never hinged copies are rare, much harder to find than survey results indicate.

Premium Characteristics
Sound condition, large balanced margins, strong color, lightly hinged or never hinged original gum, if unused; neat, non-obliterative cancel, if used. Premium copies are very difficult. The illustrated example is a gem.

Caveats
Beware faults and repairs, including regumming and reperfing. Certificate recommended in general; essential for never hinged copies and those on cover.

$2 ORANGE BROWN
YEAR OF ISSUE: 1898
SCOTT NO. 293

Scarcity
Quantity Issued: 56,200
★ Average No./Auction: 2.20
⊚ Average No./Auction: .62

Hinging
NH: 2.3%
Hinged: 97.7%

Comments
A very scarce stamp, whose small population makes it exceedingly

difficult to locate in premium condition either unused or used. This stamp is small margined and notoriously poorly centered. Faults are commonplace. Regumming and reperfing are frequently encountered. Used copies are usually heavily cancelled. Gum is typically heavily hinged or disturbed. Never hinged copies are rare. Approximately the same number were printed as for the one-dollar value, however, this stamp appears less frequently at auction, especially used.

Premium Characteristics
Sound condition, large balanced margins, fresh color, lightly hinged or never hinged original gum, if unused; neat, non-obliterative cancel, if used. Premium copies are rare. The illustrated example is a gem.

Caveats
Beware faults and repairs, including regumming and reperfing. Certificate recommended in general; essential for never hinged copies and those on cover.

PAN AMERICAN SERIES OF 1901
GENERAL COMMENTS
SCOTT NOS. 294-99

Scarcity
Quantity Issued:

No. 294	(1c)	91,401,500
No. 295	(2c)	209,759,700
No. 296	(4c)	5,737,100
No. 297	(5c)	7,201,300
No. 298	(8c)	4,921,700
No. 299	(10c)	5,043,700

General Comments
This series tends to be small margined as the above illustration of typical copies reveals. Gum is typically heavily hinged or disturbed. Faults are commonplace. Irregular perfs are frequently encountered and not considered a fault.
Used copies of the 1- and 2-cent values are abundant used; premium copies are easy to find. Used copies of the other values, while not scarce, are typically heavily canceled, poorly centered, or faulty. Premium copies of the upper values require some diligence.
Never hinged copies, while not plentiful, are much more abundant than those of nineteenth century issues. Regumming and reperfing are often encountered on

the higher values of the series. Carefully examine copies offered as never hinged.

ONE CENT. Premium copies, unused or used, are not difficult.
TWO CENT. Premium copies, unused or used, are not difficult.
FOUR CENT. Premium copies, unused or used, are not difficult.
FIVE CENT. Premium copies, unused or used, are not difficult.
EIGHT CENT. Premium unused copies are moderately difficult.
TEN CENT. Premium unused copies are moderately difficult.

Premium Characteristics
Sound condition, balanced margins (jumbo margined copies are prized and worth a substantial premium), fresh color, never hinged (light hinge okay on upper values), if unused; neat, non-obliterative cancel, if used.

Caveats
Beware faults and repairs, including regumming and reperfing, even on the lower values. Certificate recommended for more expensive never hinged premium copies.

SERIES OF 1902-3
GENERAL COMMENTS
SCOTT NOS. 300-13

Scarcity
Quantity Issued:

No. 300	(1c)	1,000,000,000 est.
No. 301	(2c)	3,261,541,426 est.
No. 302	(3c)	276,212,074
No. 303	(4c)	346,660,000 est.
No. 304	(5c)	550,320,000 est.
No. 305	(6c)	117,567,474
No. 306	(8c)	176,841,474
No. 307	(10c)	260,010,574
No. 308	(13c)	31,290,174
No. 309	(15c)	41,205,754
No. 310	(50c)	2,651,774
No. 311	($1)	504,374
No. 312	($2)	37,872
No. 313	($5)	49,211

General Comments
Stamps of this series are typically small margined and poorly centered. Gum is usually heavily hinged or disturbed. Faults are commonplace. Irregular perfs are frequently encountered and not considered a fault.

Copies above the 2-cent value are notorious for heavy cancels, however, the population below the dollar values is sufficiently abundant to make premium used copies fairly easy.

Today's never hinged stock typically comes from blocks, therefore, the low values are more abundant than the high values.

Knowledgeable buyers look for fresh,boldly colored examples and avoid those on toned paper.

ONE CENT (No. 300). Premium unused copies are not difficult.

TWO CENT No. 301). Premium unused copies are not difficult.

THREE CENT (No. 302). Premium unused copies are moderately difficult.

FOUR CENT (No. 303). Premium unused copies are moderately difficult.

FIVE CENT (No. 304). Premium unused copies are moderately difficult.

SIX CENT (no. 305). Color often poor. Vividly colored copies are prized. Premium unused copies are moderately difficult.

EIGHT CENT (No. 306). Premium unused copies are moderately difficult.

TEN CENT (No. 307). Premium unused copies are moderately difficult.

THIRTEEN CENT (No. 308). Premium unused copies are moderately difficult.

FIFTEEN CENT (No. 309). Premium unused copies are difficult.

Individual high values are covered in more detail following this section.

Premium Characteristics
Sound condition, balanced margins (jumbo margined copies are prized and worth a substantial premium), fresh color, lightly hinged or never hinged; if unused; neat, non-obliterative cancel, if used. Obtaining unused copies possessing all the premium elements is frustratingly difficult.

Caveats
Beware faults and repairs, including regumming and reperfing. Certificate recommended for never hinged, especially on the more expensive stamps of the series.

Examples of gem quality margins and centering.

50c ORANGE
YEAR OF ISSUE: 1903
SCOTT NO. 310

Scarcity
Quantity Issued: 2,651,774
★ Average No./Auction: .86

Hinging
NH: 11.8%
Hinged: 88.2%

Comments
Refer to the general comments on page 104. Color is often poor. Fresh, brightly colored copies are very scarce and command a premium. Regumming and reperfing are often encountered. The photo illustrates typical size of margins. Centering on the illustrated examples is a bit better than usually encountered.

Premium Characteristics
Sound condition, balanced margins, bright color, lightly hinged or never hinged original gum, if unused; neat, non-obliterative cancel, if used. Premium unused copies are difficult; premium used copies, although not expensive, are surprisingly difficult.

Caveats
Beware faults and repairs, including regumming and reperfing. Certificate recommended for never hinged.

$1 BLACK
YEAR OF ISSUE: 1903
SCOTT NO. 311

Scarcity
Quantity Issued: 504,374
★ Average No./Auction: 1.14
⊙ Average No./Auction: .17

Hinging
NH: 10.6%
Hinged: 89.4%

Comments
Refer to the general comments on page 104. Regumming and reperfing are frequently encountered. Never hinged copies are very scarce. The photo illustrates typical size of margins and various degrees of centering.

Premium Characteristics
Sound condition, balanced margins, strong color, lightly hinged or never hinged original gum, if unused; neat, non-obliterative cancel, if used. Premium copies are difficult.

Caveats
Beware faults and repairs, including regumming and reperfing. Certificate strongly recommended for never hinged copies and those on cover.

$2 BLUE
YEAR OF ISSUE: 1903
SCOTT NO. 312

Scarcity
Quantity Issued: 37,872
★ Average No./Auction: 1.00
⊚ Average No./Auction: .28

Hinging
NH: 8.2%
Hinged: 91.8%

Comments
Refer to the general comments on page 104. A very scarce stamp, whose small population makes it exceedingly difficult to locate in

premium condition either unused or used. It is rare never hinged. The photo illustrates typical size of margins and various degrees of centering.

Premium Characteristics
Sound condition, balanced margins, fresh color, lightly hinged or never hinged original gum, if unused; lightly canceled, if used. Premium copies are very rare.

Caveats
Beware faults and repairs, including regumming and reperfing. Although not a great problem, beware fakes made from Scott No. 479. Certificate recommended in general, and essential for never hinged and those on cover.

$5 DARK GREEN
YEAR OF ISSUE: 1903
SCOTT NO. 313

Scarcity
Quantity Issued: 49,211
★ Average No./Auction: .85
⊚ Average No./Auction: .38

Hinging
NH: 6.0%
Hinged: 94.0%

Comments
Refer to the general comments on page 104. A very scarce stamp, whose small population makes it exceedingly difficult to locate in premium condition either unused or

used. It is notoriously poorly centered. Used copies are almost always heavily cancelled. Never hinged copies are very rare. The photo illustrates typical size of margins and various degrees of centering.

Premium Characteristics
Sound condition, balanced margins, strong color, lightly hinged or never hinged original gum, if unused; lightly canceled, if used. Premium copies are exceedingly difficult.

Caveats
Beware faults and repairs, including regumming and reperfing. Although not a great problem, beware fakes made from Scott No. 480. Certificate recommended in general, and essential for never hinged copies and those on cover.

5c BLUE, Imperf.
YEAR OF ISSUE: 1908
SCOTT NO. 315

Scarcity
Quantity Issued: 4,000 est.
★ Average No./Auction: .50
⊚ Average No./Auction: .06

Hinging
NH: 25.4%
Hinged: 74.6%

Comments
This stamp should always be bought in pairs or multiples. Unused singles (except margin copies with large selvedge) should be regarded with suspicion unless certified. Genuinely used copies are very rare; an abundance of fakes exists. Used singles should be regarded as bogus unless certified. Being imperforate, pairs are usually adequately, if not nicely, margined and centered. Faults are frequently encountered, usually from hinging. Gum is typically heavily hinged or disturbed. Never hinged copies are not common, however, neither are they rare, as the auction statistic indicates. They typically result from the lower pair being severed from a block. Deep rich color is prized.

Premium Characteristics
Sound condition, large balanced margins, fresh color, never hinged original gum, if unused; light cancel of the period, if used. Premium copies are not difficult.

Caveats
Beware faults and repairs, including regumming. Beware fake cancellations. Regard singles as bogus unless certified. Certificate recommended for never hinged, and essential for used copies.

1c BLUE GREEN, Coil, perf. 12 Hz.
YEAR OF ISSUE: 1908
SCOTT NO. 316

Scarcity
Quantity Issued: very rare
★ Average No./Auction: .00

Comments
A extraordinarily rare stamp, whose minuscule population makes it exceedingly difficult to locate in any condition. In fact, none were encountered in the auction survey. This stamp is typically poorly centered. Never hinged copies, if they exist, are exceedingly rare. It is frequently faked. Used copies are almost always fakes (the illustrated example is a fake with dangerously convincing margins). Note: No genuine copies were available for illustration.

Premium Characteristics
The rarity of this stamp does not permit selectivity in the normal sense.

Caveats
Beware fakes. Certificate absolutely essential.

5c BLUE, Coil, perf. 12 Hz.
YEAR OF ISSUE: 1908
SCOTT NO. 317

Scarcity
Quantity Issued: very rare
★ Average No./Auction: .06

Hinging
NH: 00.0%
Hinged:100.0%

Comments
A very rare stamp, whose tiny population makes it exceedingly difficult to locate in premium condition either unused or used. This stamp is typically poorly centered, with margins wider on one side than the other. Never hinged copies (especially pairs), if they exist, are very rare (no never hinged copies were encountered in the survey). This stamp is frequently faked. Used copies are almost always fakes.

Premium Characteristics
This stamp is extremely difficult to locate in any condition. Its rarity does not permit selectivity in the normal sense. The illustrated example shows typical margins and centering.

Caveats
Beware fakes. Certificate absolutely essential.

1c BLUE GREEN, Coil, Perf 12, Vt.
YEAR OF ISSUE: 1908
SCOTT NO. 318

Scarcity
Quantity Issued: very rare
★ Average No./Auction: .12
⊙ Average No./Auction: .00

Hinging
NH: 00.0%
Hinged: 100.0%

Comments
A very rare stamp, whose minuscule population makes it exceedingly difficult to locate premium condition either unused or used. This stamp is typically poorly centered as the illustration shows. Never hinged copies (especially pairs), if they exist, are exceedingly rare (no never hinged pairs were encountered in the survey). This stamp is frequently faked. Used copies are almost always fakes.

Premium Characteristics
Very difficult to locate in any condition. Its rarity does not permit selectivity in the normal sense.

Caveats
Beware fakes. Certificate absolutely essential.

2c CARMINE, Coil, perf. 12 Hz.
YEAR OF ISSUE: 1908
SCOTT NO. 321

Scarcity
Quantity Issued: very rare
★ Average No./Auction: .00

Note: The design type is illustrated for
reference only; no actual stamp was available.

Comments
A great rarity whose small population makes
it exceedingly difficult to in any condition. In
fact, no copies were encountered in the
auction survey. Never hinged copies, if they
exist, are exceedingly rare. This stamp is
frequently faked. Used copies are almost
always fakes.

Premium Characteristics
The extreme rarity of this stamp does not
permit selectivity in the normal sense.
Virtually any copy is collectible.

Caveats
Beware fakes. Certificate absolutely
essential.

2c CARMINE, Coil, Perf 12, Vrt.
YEAR OF ISSUE: 1908
SCOTT NO. 322

Scarcity
Quantity Issued: very rare
★ Average No./Auction: .07
☉ Average No./Auction: .00

Hinging
NH: 16.7%
Hinged: 83.3%

Comments
A very scarce stamp, whose small population
makes it exceedingly difficult to locate in any
condition either unused or used. It is usually
poorly centered, typically to the right. Never
hinged copies are much scarcer than the
statistic indicates. It is often faked. Regard
used copies as bogus unless certified.

Premium Characteristics
This stamp is very difficult to locate in any
condition. Its rarity does not permit selectivity
in the normal sense.

Caveats
Beware fakes. Certificate absolutely
essential.

LOUISIANA PURCHASE ISSUE OF 1904
GENERAL COMMENTS
SCOTT NOS. 323-27

Scarcity
Quantity Issued:

No. 323	(1c)	79,779,200
No. 324	(2c)	192,732,400
No. 325	(3c)	4,542,600
No. 326	(5c)	6,926,700
No. 327	(10c)	4,011,200

Comments
This series tends to be small margined as the illustration reveals. Gum is often heavily hinged or disturbed. Never hinged copies, while not plentiful, are not nearly as scarce as are earlier issues. Used copies of the 3-cent through 10-cent values, while not scarce, are typically heavily canceled, poorly centered, or faulty. Regumming and reperfing are frequently encountered on the higher values of the series.

ONE CENT & TWO CENT. Premium copies are not difficult.
THREE CENT. Premium copies are somewhat difficult, especially NH.
FIVE CENT. Premium copies are moderately difficult, especially NH.
TEN CENT. Premium copies are difficult, especially NH.

Premium Characteristics
Sound condition, balanced margins (jumbo margined copies are prized and worth a substantial premium), fresh color, never hinged, if unused; neat, non-obliterative cancel, if used.

Caveats
Beware faults and repairs, including regumming and reperfing, even on the lower values.

JAMESTOWN ISSUE OF 1907
GENERAL COMMENTS
SCOTT NOS. 328-30

Scarcity
Quantity Issued:

No. 328	(1c)	77,728,794
No. 329	(2c)	149,497,994
No. 330	(5c)	7,980,594

Comments
This series is small margined with a vengeance. The illustrated example is wonderfully margined and centered for this issue. Used copies of the 5-cent, while not scarce, are typically heavily canceled, poorly centered, or faulty. Unused copies are often heavily hinged. Never hinged copies, while not plentiful, are not difficult. Premium never hinged copies are very difficult.

Premium Characteristics
Sound condition, balanced margins (large margined copies are scarce and worth a substantial premium), fresh color, never hinged, if unused; light cancel, if used.

Caveats
Beware faults and repairs, including regumming and reperfing (only occasionally encountered and not much of a problem).

WASHINGTON-FRANKLIN SERIES OF 1908-9
Perf 12, Double Line Watermark
SCOTT NOS. 331-42

Scarcity
Quantity Issued: not known

Comments
A beautiful series plagued by a host of problems typical of the era: heavy hinging or disturbed gum, small margins, notoriously poor centering, and annoyingly frequent faults. Irregular perfs are often encountered and not considered a fault (note perfs in the photos below). Used copies are usually heavily cancelled, however, the population under the dollar value is sufficiently abundant so that premium used copies are not difficult. Most never hinged stock comes from blocks; the lower values are relatively more plentiful, but by no means abundant. Taking premium factors into account, never hinged copies are surprisingly difficult.
Knowledgeable buyers look for fresh, boldly colored examples and avoid those on toned paper.

ONE CENT (No. 331). Premium never hinged copies are not difficult.
TWO CENT (No. 332). Premium never hinged copies are not difficult.

THREE CENT (No. 333). Premium never hinged copies are moderately difficult.
FOUR CENT (No. 334). Premium never hinged copies are moderately difficult.
FIVE CENT (No. 335). Premium never hinged copies are difficult.
SIX CENT (No. 336). Color does not age well. Often turns brownish. Vividly colored copies are prized. Premium never hinged copies are moderately difficult.
EIGHT CENT (No. 337). Premium never hinged copies are moderately difficult.
TEN CENT (No. 338). Premium never hinged copies are very difficult.
THIRTEEN CENT (No. 339). Premium never hinged copies are moderately difficult.
FIFTEEN CENT (No. 340). The natural color of this stamp is pale. Strikingly colored copies rare. Premium never hinged copies are very difficult.

Premium Characteristics
Sound condition, balanced margins (jumbo margined copies are prized and worth a substantial premium), fresh color, never hinged, if unused; neat, non-obliterative cancel, if used.

Caveats
Beware faults and repairs, including regumming and reperfing. Certificate recommended for never hinged copies of the more expensive stamps of the series.

Examples of margins and centering, which, if anything, are a cut above that normally encountered.

Note margins and centering, which are about as nice as they come.

50c VIOLET, Perf 12,
Double Line Watermark
YEAR OF ISSUE: 1908-9
SCOTT NO. 341

Scarcity
Quantity Issued: 1,826,790
★ Average No./Auction: .91

Hinging
NH: 14.4%
Hinged: 85.6%

Comments
This stamp is small margined and notoriously poorly centered. The illustrated example on the left is, if anything, better centered than usual; the example on the right possesses fabulous margins and is wonderfully centered for this issue. Color is susceptible to fading and often languid. Fresh, brightly colored copies are scarce and worth a premium. Used copies are usually heavily cancelled and atrociously centered. Gum is typically heavily hinged or disturbed. Never hinged copies are scarce. Regumming is occasionally encountered.

Premium Characteristics
Sound condition, balanced margins, bright color, lightly hinged or never hinged original gum, if unused; neat, non-obliterative cancel, if used. Premium unused copies are extremely difficult (especially NH); premium used copies, although not expensive, are surprisingly difficult.

Caveats
Beware faults and repairs, including regumming and reperfing. Certificate recommended for never hinged.

$1 VIOLET BROWN, Perf 12,
Double Line Watermark
YEAR OF ISSUE: 1908-9
SCOTT NO. 342

Scarcity
Quantity Issued: 313,590
★ Average No./Auction: .89
⊙ Average No./Auction: .10

Hinging
NH: 10.2%
Hinged: 89.8%

Comments
This stamp is notoriously poorly centered, and often faulty. The illustrated example on the left is better margined and centered than usual; the example on the right is a gem. Used copies are usually heavily cancelled. Gum is typically heavily hinged or disturbed. Regumming is occasionally encountered. Never hinged copies are rare.

Premium Characteristics
Sound condition, balanced margins, strong color, lightly hinged or never hinged original gum, if unused; neat, non-obliterative cancel, if used. Premium unused copies are extremely difficult, especially NH; premium used copies are surprisingly difficult.

Caveats
Beware faults and repairs, including regumming and reperfing. Certificate recommended for never hinged.

WASHINGTON-FRANKLIN SERIES
IMPERFORATES OF 1908-9
Double Line Watermark
SCOTT NOS. 343-47

Scarcity
Quantity Issued:

No. 343	(1c)	not known
No. 344	(2c)	not known
No. 345	(3c)	not known
No. 346	(4c)	20,000 est.
No. 347	(5c)	15,000 est.

General Comments
Unlike their perforated counterparts, these imperforates are generally well centered and adequately margined. They are usually collected in pairs. Unused copies are typically hinged, often heavily; nevertheless, never hinged copies are not difficult to locate. Knowledgeable buyers look for fresh, boldly colored copies and avoid those on toned paper.

Premium Characteristics
Sound condition, large balanced margins, fresh color, never hinged. if unused; neat, non-obliterative cancel, if used.

Caveats
Regumming is encountered occasionally. Avoid single copies, unless they are margin copies with abundant selvedge.

WASHINGTON-FRANKLIN SERIES
COIL STAMPS, Perf 12, Horizontally
Double Line Watermark
SCOTT NOS. 348-51

Scarcity
Quantity Issued: not known

General Comments
These coils are generally poorly centered; it is difficult to find copies with balanced margins on all sides. Of the illustrated examples, the pair on the far left is a gem; the others are more typical of the issue, which is often centered right or left. Line pairs are particularly frustrating. Perforation separations can be a problem, most often on pairs having brittle paper. Unused copies are typically hinged, often heavily. Never hinged pairs of the 4- and 5-cent are quite scarce. Knowledgeable buyers look for fresh, boldly colored copies and avoid those on toned paper. All values are faked, as are many Washington-Franklin coils.

Premium Characteristics
Sound condition, balanced margins, fresh color, never hinged or lightly hinged, if unused; neat, non-obliterative cancel, if used. Premium copies are difficult; premium line pairs are very difficult.

Caveats
Beware fakes (this cannot be stressed strongly enough). Beware regumming. Certificate essential, especially for line pairs.

WASHINGTON-FRANKLIN COILS
Perf 12 Vertically
Double Line Watermark
SCOTT NOS. 352-56

Scarcity
Quantity Issued: not known

General Comments
These coils are generally poorly centered, typically high or low. It is difficult to find copies with balanced margins on all sides. Spacing of perf rows frequently varies from one side of a pair to the other, as the strips above illustrate. Perforation separations can be a problem due to the size of the holes. Separations are most often found on pairs having brittle paper. Gum is typically hinged, often heavily. Knowledgeable buyers look for fresh, boldly colored copies and avoid those on toned paper. CAUTION: All values are faked, as are many of the Washington-Franklin coils.

ONE & TWO CENT (No. 352-353). Premium copies are difficult, especially NH.
FOUR CENT (No. 354). Premium copies are very difficult, especially never hinged. Non-premium never hinged pairs are moderately difficult. Never hinged line pairs are extremely difficult.
FIVE CENT (No. 355). Premium copies are very difficult, especially never hinged. Non-premium never hinged pairs are moderately difficult. Never hinged line pairs are extremely difficult.
TEN CENT (No. 356). It is estimated that only about 300 unused copies reached collectors' hands. Premium copies, both unused or used, are extremely difficult. Never hinged pairs are exceedingly rare. Never hinged line pairs are of the utmost rarity. CAUTION: This stamp is *frequently* faked.

Premium Characteristics
The key to this series is centering, centering, centering. Sound copies with balanced margins, fresh color, never hinged or lightly hinged, if unused; neat, non-obliterative cancel, if used.

Caveats
Beware fakes (this cannot be stressed strongly enough). All values are frequently faked. Beware regumming. Certificate strongly recommended for all, and is essential for more expensive singles, pairs, and for all line pairs.

WASHINGTON-FRANKLIN SERIES
BLUE PAPER VARIETY
SCOTT NOS. 357-66

Scarcity
Quantity Issued:

No. 357	(1c)	1,480,000
No. 358	(2c)	1,494,000
No. 359	(3c)	4,000
No. 360	(4c)	4,000
No. 361	(5c)	4,000
No. 362	(6c)	5,200
No. 363	(8c)	4,000
No. 364	(10c)	4,000
No. 365	(13c)	4,000
No. 366	(15c)	4,000

Comments
The blue papers suffer from the same problems that plague other stamps of the era: heavy hinging or disturbed gum, small margins, and faults. They are notoriously poorly centered. Centering on the illustrated examples is quite reasonable and acceptable for the issue. Gem copies are exceedingly rare. Irregular perfs are frequently encountered and not considered a fault.
Used blue papers, typically the 1- and 2-cent values, are often faked by soaking regular stamps in blue fountain pen ink. The result is too blue; genuine blue paper is a very subtle, almost gray, shade. Straight-edged stamps comprised 19 percent of the total issued; a great many have been reperforated.

ONE CENT (No. 357). Premium copies are moderately difficult, especially NH.
TWO CENT (No. 358). Premium copies are moderately difficult, especially NH.
THREE CENT (No. 359). Very scarce unused. Rare never hinged. Premium copies are extremely difficult.
FOUR CENT (No. 360). Of the 4,000 printed, it is estimated that only about 100 were saved by collectors. Not known used. Exceedingly rare never hinged. Premium copies are exceedingly difficult.
FIVE CENT (No. 361). Very rare unused or used. Usually poorly centered. Very rare never hinged. Premium copies are extremely difficult.
SIX CENT (No. 362). One of the more common of the blue papers, nevertheless, scarce. Usually poorly centered. Very rare never hinged. Premium copies are extremely difficult.
EIGHT CENT (No. 363). Of the 4,000 printed, it is estimated that only about 90-100 were saved by collectors. Usually poorly centered. Not known used. Exceedingly rare never hinged. Premium copies are exceedingly difficult.
TEN CENT (No. 364). Very scarce unused and very rare used. Usually poorly centered. Very rare never hinged. Premium copies are exceedingly difficult.
THIRTEEN CENT (No. 365). Of the 4,000 printed, it is estimated that only a few hundred were saved by collectors. Used copies exist but are rare. Usually poorly centered. Very rare never hinged. Premium copies are exceedingly difficult.
FIFTEEN CENT (No. 366). Among the more commonly encountered blue papers, although still very scarce unused or used. Usually poorly centered. Rare never hinged. Premium copies are exceedingly difficult.

Premium Characteristics
Sound condition, balanced margins, fresh color, lightly hinged or never hinged, if unused; lightly canceled, if used.

Caveats
Beware faults and repairs, including regumming and reperfing. Certificate essential.

THE 1909 COMMEMORATIVES
GENERAL COMMENTS
SCOTT NOS. 367-71

Scarcity
Quantity Issued:

No. 367	(2c Lincoln)	148,387,191
No. 368	(Lincoln imperf)	1,273,900
No. 369	(Lincoln blue paper)	637,000
No. 370	(2c Alaska)	152,887,311
No. 371	(Alaska imperf)	525,400
No. 372	(2c Hudson-Fulton)	72,634,631
No. 373	(Hudson-Fulton imperf)	216,480

Comments
The perforated 2-cent Lincoln (No. 367) is typically poorly centered, but a large population exists, so nicely centered copies can be found. The perforated Alaska-Yukon and Hudson-Fulton stamps (Nos. 370 and 372) possess larger margins (as can be seen on the illustrated imperf pairs above); therefore, visually appealing copies are not too difficult.

All the imperforates are generally well centered. Used singles are frequently faked by trimming perfs off. As with all imperfs, it is wise to be suspicious of singles, except margin copies with adequate selvedge.

Hinged copies are generally heavily hinged, although adequate stocks of never hinged exist and are readily available. Stamps of these issues are frequently toned from storage in old-time stockbooks. Knowledgeable buyers look for fresh copies and avoid those on toned paper.

TWO CENT LINCOLN BLUE PAPER (No. 369).
Usually poorly centered, however, nicely centered copies do exist, mostly from the 3mm spacing variety. The two illustrated examples on the top row show variations in margins and centering; they are better than typically encountered. The one at lower left is a gem. Used copies are occasionally faked using dilute blue fountain pen ink. Genuine blue paper is a subtle, almost gray shade, best observed from the back. Beware reperfed straightedged copies. Premium copies are moderately difficult.

Premium Characteristics
Sound condition, balance margins, fresh color, never hinged, if unused (lightly hinged Scott No. 369s are acceptable); light cancel, if used. Premium copies are not difficult, except the 2-cent Lincoln blue paper (No. 369), which is moderately difficult.

Caveats
Be aware that regumming is encountered occasionally, mostly on the imperfs and Lincoln blue paper. Beware fake used Lincoln blue papers. Beware used imperf singles.

WASHINGTON-FRANKLIN SERIES
Perf 12, Single Line Watermark
SCOTT NOS. 374-82

Scarcity
Quantity Issued: not known

Comments
This series is plagued by the same problems that afflict their double line watermarked counterparts: heavy hinging or disturbed gum, small margins, notoriously poor centering, and annoyingly frequent faults. Irregular perfs are often encountered and not considered a fault.
It is easier to locate never hinged copies than nicely centered copies. Never hinged copies with balanced margins are scarce, indeed. Never hinged jumbo margined copies are extremely difficult, but highly prized and worth a substantial premium. The stamp on the left is a jumbo margined gem. The three stamps on the right illustrate centering characteristic of this series.
Used copies are usually heavily cancelled, however, the population is sufficiently large so that premium used copies are not difficult.

ONE CENT (No. 374). Premium copies are not difficult.
TWO CENT (No. 375). Premium copies are not difficult.

THREE CENT (No. 376). Vivid color prized. Premium copies not difficult.
FOUR CENT (No. 377). Warm, rich browns prized. Notoriously poorly centered. Premium copies are moderately difficult.
FIVE CENT (No. 378). Intense color prized. Usually poorly centered. Premium copies are moderately difficult.
SIX CENT (No. 379). Color susceptible to browning. Fresh, bright color prized. Premium copies are difficult.
EIGHT CENT (No. 380). Color often not pronounced. Rich color prized. Premium copies are difficult.
TEN CENT (No. 381). Rich, deeply colored copies prized. Premium copies are difficult.
FIFTEEN CENT (No. 382). Color naturally pale. Brilliantly colored copies prized. Scarce never hinged. Premium copies are very difficult.

Premium Characteristics
Sound condition, balanced margins (jumbo margined copies are worth a substantial premium), fresh color, never hinged, if unused; light cancel, if used. Copies possessing all the premium characteristics are very scarce.

Caveats
Beware faults and repairs, including regumming and reperfing. Certificate recommended for gum, especially on the more expensive values.

Natural inclusions (wood fibers, carbon specks, etc.) were inherent in the manufacture of paper used for certain issues such as the Columbians, Trans-Mississippis, Panama-Pacifics, and Washington-Franklins. They are especially noticeable on yellow, red and orange stamps. While aesthetically distracting, they should not be considered faults, *per se.*

**WASHINGTON-FRANKLIN COILS
Perf 12 Horizontally,
Single Line Watermark
SCOTT NOS. 385-86**

Scarcity
Quantity Issued: not known

General Comments
Like all Washington-Franklins, centering is the most difficult element of condition, although these coils are not as uniformly poorly centered as the previous coil issue (Scott Nos 348-49). Gum is typically heavily hinged or disturbed. Faults are commonplace. Irregular perfs are frequently encountered and not considered a fault. Pairs occasionally have separated perfs. Never hinged copies exist and are fairly easy to locate. Never hinged line pairs are much more difficult. Never hinged copies with balanced margins are very scarce. Like most coils of this era, these are frequently faked.

Premium Characteristics
Sound condition, balanced margins, fresh color, never hinged, if unused; light cancel, if used.

Caveats
Beware fakes. Certificate recommended, essential for line pairs.

**WASHINGTON-FRANKLIN COILS
Perf 12 Vertically,
Single Line Watermark
SCOTT NOS. 387-88**

Scarcity
Quantity Issued: not known

General Comments
The perf 12 vertically, single line watermarked coils are much scarcer than their horizontally perforated counterparts. Like all Washington-Franklins, centering is the most difficult element of condition. Gum is typically heavily hinged or disturbed. Faults are commonplace. Irregular perfs are frequently encountered and not considered a fault. Pairs occasionally have separated perfs. Like most coils of this era, they are frequently faked.
Exists with either 2mm or 3mm spacing.

ONE CENT (No. 387). Scarce never hinged. Frequently faked. Premium copies very scarce, especially never hinged.
TWO CENT (No. 388). Rare never hinged. Often encountered with faults. Frequently faked. Premium copies are exceedingly rare. Genuine line pairs are among the rarest items of twentieth century U.S. philately. The illustrated pair is centered high, as often.

Premium Characteristics
Sound copies with balanced margins, fresh color, never hinged or lightly hinged, if unused; light cancel, if used.

Caveats
Beware fakes. Certificate essential, especially for line pairs.

**WASHINGTON-FRANKLIN
"ORANGEBURG COIL"
3c DEEP VIOLET, Perf 12 Vertically
Single Line Watermark
YEAR OF ISSUE: 1911
SCOTT NO. 389**

Scarcity
Quantity Issued: 100 est.
⊙ Average No./Auction: .06

Comments
The "Orangeburg coil" is one of the great
U.S. rarities. Used copies typically possess a
wavy line cancel (the existence of unused
copies is questioned). Most copies are poorly
centered. Often faulty. This coil is frequently
faked.

Premium Characteristics
The population of this rarity is too restricted to
permit selectivity in the normal sense. It is
difficult to locate in any condition.

Caveats
Beware fakes. Certificate absolutely
essential.

**WASHINGTON-FRANKLIN COILS
PERF 8½ Horizontally,
Single Line Watermark
SCOTT NOS. 390-91**

Scarcity
Quantity Issued: not known

Comments
Perforations are usually very irregular. The
perf tips on the illustrated examples are
typical, and if anything, better than usual for
this issue. Finding nicely centered copies is
much easier than finding copies with cleanly
separated, uniform perforations. The 2-cent
is more difficult to find nicely centered than
the 1-cent. Frequently with faults. Pairs
possessing brittle paper tend to have weak
perfs. Typically hinged, often heavily;
nevertheless, never hinged copies exist and
are fairly easy to locate.   Never hinged line
pairs, especially the 2-cent (Scott No. 391),
are much more difficult. Line pairs are faked
just frequently enough to be a nuisance.

Premium Characteristics
Sound condition, balanced margins, fresh
color, even perforations, never hinged, if
unused; light cancel, if used.

Caveats
Beware faked line pairs. Certificate
recommended for line pairs of Scott No. 391.

WASHINGTON-FRANKLIN COILS
PERF 8½ Vertically,
Single Line Watermark
SCOTT NOS. 392-96

Scarcity
Quantity Issued: not known

General Comments
These stamps are widely margined (the 3-cent and 4-cent also exist with narrower 2mm spacing). Irregular perfs are standard for this issue and not considered a fault. Perfs on the illustrated examples are typical of what you can expect. Anything nicer is a bonus. These coils are so hard to separate cleanly that pairs were sometimes cut apart (retaining parts of adjoining stamps, as in the illustration) in order to preserve the perfs. It is easier to find never hinged or nicely centered stamps than those with uniformly separated perfs. Centering varies as is apparent on the strip of four.
Faults are commonplace. Pairs with brittle paper tend to have weak perfs. Typically hinged, often lightly, sometimes heavily. Never hinged copies are not terribly difficult to locate for the two lower values of the series. Never hinged copies of the three upper values are somewhat scarcer. Never hinged line pairs are much more difficult, especially for the top three values of the series. Check line pairs carefully for signs of tampering.
ONE CENT (No. 392). Pairs and line pairs not difficult in premium condition.

Frequently faked, especially line pairs.
TWO CENT (No. 393). Pairs not difficult in premium condition. Line pairs moderately difficult. Frequently faked, especially line pairs.
THREE CENT (No. 394). Typically hinged, and more difficult never hinged than the two low values of the series. Line pairs are scarce never hinged. Seldom faked. Line pairs are fairly difficult in premium condition.
FOUR CENT (No. 395). Typically hinged, and more difficult never hinged than the two low values of the series. Line pairs are scarce never hinged. This stamp is not faked, however, line pairs occasionally are and should be checked carefully. Line pairs are fairly difficult in premium condition.
FIVE CENT (No. 396). Typically hinged, and more difficult never hinged than the two low values of the series. Line pairs are scarce never hinged. This stamp is not faked, however, line pairs occasionally are and should be checked carefully. Line pairs are fairly difficult in premium condition.

Premium Characteristics
Sound condition, balanced margins, cleanly separated, uniform perforations, fresh color, never hinged, if unused; light cancel, if used.

Caveats
Beware fakes, especially line pairs. Beware regumming. Certificate essential for line pairs.

PANAMA PACIFIC SERIES OF 1904
Perf 12
SCOTT NOS. 397-400A

Scarcity
Quantity Issued: not known

General Comments
The spacing between stamps is fairly
wide, however, the spacing of perf rows
is inconsistent, yielding both large and
small margined copies, as illustrated on
the top row. Centering also varies quite a
bit. Nicely centered copies of the 1- and
2-cent are not difficult. Nicely centered
copies of the 5- and 10-cent are much
more difficult, especially the 10-cent,
which is typically off center as the
illustration shows.
Gum is often heavily hinged or disturbed.
Nicely centered, never hinged copies of
the three high values are very tough.
The 1- and 2-cent values are abundant
used; premium copies are easy to find.
Used copies of the 5- and 10-cent values,
while not scarce, are typically heavily
canceled, poorly centered, or faulty.
Inclusions are often encountered (refer to
the note at the bottom of page 117).
They can be very distracting on the 10-
cent values. Regumming and reperfing
are encountered just frequently enough to
merit caution.

ONE CENT (No. 397). Premium copies are
not difficult.
TWO CENT (No. 398). Premium copies are
not difficult.
FIVE CENT (No. 399). Moderately scarce
never hinged. Exists in deep rich shades
that are very striking. Premium copies
are moderately difficult, especially never
hinged.
TEN CENT ORANGE YELLOW (No. 400).
Typically hinged, often heavily. Usually
poorly centered. Moderately scarce
never hinged. Premium copies are
difficult, especially never hinged.
TEN CENT ORANGE (No. 400A). Typically
hinged, often heavily. Usually poorly
centered. Scarce never hinged.
Premium copies are much more difficult
than Scott No. 400, especially never
hinged.

Premium Characteristics
Sound condition, balanced margins
(jumbo margined copies are prized and
worth a substantial premium), fresh color,
never hinged, if unused; light cancel, if
used.

Caveats
Beware faults and repairs, including
regumming and reperfing. Certificate
recommended for more expensive
premium copies.

PANAMA PACIFIC SERIES OF 1904
Perf 10
SCOTT NOS. 401-404

Scarcity
Quantity Issued: not known

General Comments
This series is widely margined, however centering is much more difficult than on the previous perf 12 issue (Nos. 397-400A). Nicely centered copies of the 1- and 2-cent, while not rare, require some effort to find. Nicely centered copies of the 5- and 10-cent values are a real challenge, especially the 10-cent. Irregular perfs are typical, as on all of perf 10s. The illustrated examples are quite characteristic of the issue.
Gum is often heavily hinged or disturbed. Nicely centered, never hinged copies of the high values are tough.
The 1- and 2-cent values are abundant used; premium copies are fairly easy to find. Used copies of the 5- and 10-cent values, while not scarce, are typically heavily canceled, poorly centered, or faulty.
Inclusions are frequently encountered on this series (refer to the note at the bottom of page 117). They can be very distracting on the 10-cent value. Regumming and reperfing are encountered just frequently enough on the 5- and 10-cent values to merit caution.

ONE CENT (No. 401). Premium copies are moderately difficult.
TWO CENT (No. 402). Premium copies are moderately difficult.
FIVE CENT (No. 403). Typically hinged, often heavily. Moderately scarce never hinged. Usually poorly centered. Premium copies are difficult, especially never hinged.
TEN CENT (No. 404). Typically hinged, often heavily. Scarce never hinged (much more scarce than the perf 12 variety). Usually poorly centered. Premium copies are extremely difficult, especially never hinged.

Premium Characteristics
Sound condition, balanced margins (jumbo margined copies are prized and worth a substantial premium), fresh color, never hinged (lightly hinged acceptable on the 10-cent value), if unused; light cancel, if used.

Caveats
Beware faults and repairs, including regumming and reperfing. Certificate recommended for more expensive unused premium copies, especially never hinged.

**WASHINGTON-FRANKLIN SERIES
Perf 12, Single Line Watermark
SCOTT NOS. 405-07**

Scarcity
Quantity Issued: not known

General Comments
Typically small margined and poorly centered, as is characteristic of perf 12s. Typically hinged, often heavily.

ONE & TWO CENT (Nos. 405-06). Large population exists. Not difficult never hinged or in premium condition.
SEVEN CENT (No. 407). Typically poorly centered and hinged. Premium copies are moderately difficult.

Premium Characteristics
Sound condition, balanced margins (jumbo margined copies are worth a substantial premium), fresh color, never hinged, if unused; light cancel, if used.

Caveats
Beware faults and repairs, including regumming and reperfing. Certificate suggested for unused premium copies of Scott No. 407.

**WASHINGTON-FRANKLIN COILS
Perf 8½ Horizontally,
Single Line Watermark
SCOTT NOS. 410-11**

Scarcity
Quantity Issued: not known

Comments
Refer to page 119 and the general comments and illustrations for Scott Nos. 390-91 regarding perfs and centering. Typically hinged, often heavily, although never hinged copies are not particularly scarce. Despite being relatively inexpensive,

these coils are frequently faked, especially line pairs, which catalogue much more than plain pairs.

Premium Characteristics
Sound condition, balanced margins, fresh color, reasonably uniform perforations, never hinged, if unused; light cancel, if used. Premium copies are not difficult (reasonably uniform perfs are the toughest premium element).

Caveats
Beware fakes, especially used line pairs. This issue is frequently faked. Certificate recommended for premium copies.

**WASHINGTON-FRANKLIN COILS
Perf 8½ Vertically,
Single Line Watermark
SCOTT NOS. 412-13**

Scarcity
Quantity Issued: not known

Comments
Refer to page 120 and the general comments and illustrations for Scott Nos. 392-93 regarding perfs and centering. Typically hinged, often heavily, although never hinged copies are not particularly scarce. Despite being relatively inexpensive, these

coils are frequently faked, especially line pairs, which catalogue much more than plain pairs.

Premium characteristics
Sound condition, balanced margins, fresh color, reasonably uniform perforations, never hinged, if unused; light cancel, if used. Premium copies of No. 412 are not terribly difficult. No. 413 is scarcer and more difficult, especially lines pairs.

Caveats
Beware fakes, especially used line pairs. This issue is frequently faked. Certificate recommended for line pairs.

WASHINGTON-FRANKLIN SERIES
Perf 12, Single Line Watermark
SCOTT NOS. 414-21

Scarcity
Quantity Issued: not known

General Comments
These stamps are plagued by the same problems that afflict the other perf 12 Washington-Franklins: heavy hinging or disturbed gum, small margins, notoriously poor centering, and annoyingly frequent faults. Irregular perfs are often encountered and not considered a fault. Never hinged copies are easier to locate than nicely centered ones. Never hinged copies with balanced margins are difficult, indeed. Never hinged jumbo margined copies are extremely difficult, but highly prized and worth a substantial premium. The illustrated examples give an idea of characteristic margins and centering for the series, and, if anything, are better than ordinarily encountered.
Used copies are usually heavily cancelled.
Refer to the note regarding inclusions at the bottom of page 117.

EIGHT CENT (No. 414). Premium copies are difficult, especially never hinged.
NINE CENT (No. 415). Premium copies are difficult, especially never hinged.
TEN CENT (No. 416). Premium copies are difficult, especially never hinged.
TWELVE CENT (No. 417). Premium copies are difficult, especially never hinged.
FIFTEEN CENT (No. 418). Premium copies are difficult, especially never hinged.
TWENTY CENT (No. 419). Premium copies are very difficult, especially never hinged.
THIRTY CENT (No. 420). Premium copies are very difficult, especially never hinged.

Premium Characteristics
Sound condition, balanced margins (jumbo margined copies are worth a substantial premium), fresh color, never hinged (or lightly hinged for the more expensive values), if unused; light cancel, if used.

Caveats
Beware faults and repairs, including regumming and reperfing. Certificate recommended for gum, especially on the more expensive values.

**50c VIOLET, Perf 12,
Single Line Watermark**
YEAR OF ISSUE: 1914
SCOTT NO. 421

Scarcity
Quantity Issued: not known
★ Average No./Auction: .72

Hinging
NH: 26.8%
Hinged: 73.2%

Comments
Refer to the general comments for the series on page 124. It's violet color is susceptible to fading. Fresh, lustrously colored copies are scarce and command a premium. All genuine copies have natural offset on the reverse (the offset is on the paper, not the gum). Used copies are usually heavily cancelled and atrociously centered. Gum is typically heavily hinged or disturbed. Regumming is frequent enough to be a problem. The illustrated example on the left is somewhat better than typically encountered; the example on the right is a large margined gem.

Premium Characteristics
Sound condition, balanced margins (jumbo margined copies are worth a substantial premium), bright color, never hinged original gum, if unused; light cancel, if used. Premium unused copies are extremely difficult; premium used copies, although not expensive, are surprisingly difficult.

Caveats
Beware faults and repairs, including regumming and reperfing. Certificate recommended for never hinged.

**50c VIOLET, Perf 12,
Double Line Watermark**
YEAR OF ISSUE: 1912
SCOTT NO. 422

Scarcity
Quantity Issued: not known
★ Average No./Auction: .70

Hinging
NH: 14.5%
Hinged: 85.5%

Comments
Refer to the general comments for the series on page 124. No printing offset is found on this stamp (those with offset are Scott No. 421). Used copies are usually heavily cancelled and atrociously centered. Gum is typically heavily hinged or disturbed. Regumming is frequent enough to be a problem. The illustrated example on the left is somewhat better than typically encountered; the example on the right is a large margined gem.

Premium Characteristics
Sound condition, balanced margins (jumbo margined copies are worth a substantial premium), bright color, never hinged original gum, if unused; light cancel, if used. Premium unused copies are extremely difficult (although not as difficult as Scott No. 421); premium used copies, although not expensive, are surprisingly difficult.

Caveats
Beware faults and repairs, including regumming and reperfing. Certificate recommended for never hinged.

$1 VIOLET BROWN, Perf 12,
Double Line Watermark
YEAR OF ISSUE: 1912
SCOTT NO. 423

Scarcity
Quantity Issued: not known
★ Average No./Auction: .87

Hinging
NH: 15.1%
Hinged: 84.9%

Comments
Refer to the general comments on
page 124. Fresh, brightly colored
copies are scarce and command a premium.
Used copies are usually heavily cancelled
and atrociously centered. Gum is typically
heavily hinged or disturbed. Regumming is
frequent enough to be a problem. The
illustrated example on the left shows typical
centering; the one on the right is a beautifully
margined gem.

Premium Characteristics
Sound condition, balanced margins (jumbo
margined copies are worth a considerable
premium), bright color, never hinged original
gum, if unused; light cancel, if used.
Premium unused copies are extremely
difficult; premium used copies, although only
moderately expensive, are surprisingly
difficult.

Caveats
Beware faults and repairs, including
regumming and reperfing. Certificate
recommended for never hinged.

50c VIOLET, Perf 10,
Single Line Watermark
YEAR OF ISSUE: 1915
SCOTT NO. 440

Scarcity
Quantity Issued: not known
★ Average No./Auction: .74

Hinging
NH: 17.8%
Hinged: 82.2%

Comments
Refer to the general comments on
page 127. The violet is susceptible to
fading; avoid continuous exposure to
light. It is also reported that some
watermark fluids may affect the
pigment. Fresh, lustrously colored
copies are scarce and command a
premium. Irregular perfs are endemic and not
considered a fault. Used copies are usually
heavily canceled and atrociously centered.
Gum is typically hinged, often heavily.
Regumming is frequent enough to be a
problem. The illustrated example on the left
shows typical margins and, perhaps,
somewhat better than average centering; the
one on the right is wonderfully centered.
Note the perfs on both stamps, which are
typical for this issue and perfectly acceptable.

Premium Characteristics
Sound condition, balanced margins (jumbo
margined copies command a substantial
premium), bright color, never hinged original
gum, if unused. Premium unused copies are
exceedingly difficult; premium used copies,
although not expensive, are surprisingly
difficult. Never hinged copies with large
balanced margins are almost impossible to
find.

Caveats
Beware faults and repairs, including
regumming and reperfing. Certificate
recommended for gum, especially never
hinged.

WASHINGTON-FRANKLIN SERIES
Perf 10, Single Line Watermark
SCOTT NOS. 424-40

Scarcity
Quantity Issued: not known

General Comments
These stamps are notoriously poorly centered (the illustrated examples possess much better centering than normally encountered). Irregular perfs are to be expected and not considered a fault; that's just the way they come. Note the condition of the perfs, which are typical, on the illustrated examples; they are perfectly acceptable. Gum is usually hinged, often heavily, or disturbed. Faults, frequently hinge thins, are commonplace.

Never hinged copies are easier to locate than nicely centered ones or those with uniform perfs.

Refer to the note regarding inclusions at the bottom of page 117.

ONE CENT (No. 424). Premium copies are not difficult.

TWO CENT (No. 425). Premium copies are not difficult.

THREE CENT (No. 426). Premium copies are moderately difficult.

FOUR CENT (No. 427). Premium copies are moderately difficult.

FIVE CENT (No. 428). Premium copies are moderately difficult.

SIX CENT (No. 429). Color subject to chemical change (browning). Premium copies are difficult.

SEVEN CENT (No. 430). Premium copies are very difficult, especially never hinged.

EIGHT CENT (No. 431). Premium copies are very difficult, especially never hinged.

NINE CENT (No. 432). Premium copies are very difficult, especially never hinged.

TEN CENT (No. 433). Premium copies are very difficult, especially never hinged.

ELEVEN CENT (No. 434). Premium copies are very difficult, especially never hinged.

TWELVE CENT (No. 435). Premium copies are very difficult, especially never hinged.

FIFTEEN CENT (No. 437). Usually a pale, low contrast shade. Deep rich color is prized. Premium copies are very difficult, especially never hinged.

TWENTY CENT (No. 438). Premium copies are extremely difficult, especially NH.

THIRTY CENT (No. 439). Premium copies are extremely difficult, especially NH. Refer to page 126 for Scott No. 440.

Premium Characteristics
Sound condition, balanced margins (jumbo margined copies are worth a substantial premium), reasonably uniform perfs, fresh color, never hinged, if unused; light cancel, if used.

Never hinged copies with balanced margins and uniform perfs are almost impossible, especially the higher values.

Caveats
Beware faults and repairs, including regumming and reperfing. Certificate recommended for never hinged, more expensive values.

WASHINGTON-FRANKLIN COILS
Perf 10 Horizontally,
Single Line Watermark
SCOTT NOS. 441-2

Scarcity
Quantity Issued: not known

Comments
These stamps are often poorly
centered. Of the illustrated examples,
the one on the left is nicely centered
for this issue; the one on the right is
more typical of what to expect.
Irregular perfs are characteristic of
perf 10s, and not considered a fault.

Those in the illustration are typical.
Occasionally, pairs are seen clipped apart,
retaining parts of adjoining stamps, in order to
preserve the perfs.
Copies are typically hinged, sometimes
heavily, however, a sufficient population
exists so that never hinged copies are fairly
easy to find.

ONE CENT (No. 441). Perfs more difficult than
centering. Infrequently faked, however,
buyers should scrutinize line pairs. Premium
copies are not difficult.
TWO CENT (No. 442). Perfs more difficult than
centering. Frequently faked, and dangerous
because the stamp is too inexpensive to
justify the cost of certification. Buyers should
scrutinize line pairs carefully. Premium
copies are not difficult.

Premium Characteristics
Sound condition, balanced margins, fresh
color, reasonably uniform perforations, never
hinged, if unused; light cancel, if used.

Caveats
Beware fakes of No. 442, especially line
pairs. Certificate suggested for premium
copies.

WASHINGTON-FRANKLIN COILS
Perf 10 Vertically,
Single Line Watermark
SCOTT NOS. 443-47

Scarcity
Quantity Issued: not known

General Comments
These stamps are usually poorly centered. The line pair at bottom right is an exceptional gem; the other pairs illustrate centering more typical of the issue. Irregular perfs are characteristic of perf 10s, and not considered a fault. Note the condition of perfs in the illustration. Occasionally, pairs are seen clipped apart, retaining parts of adjoining stamps in order to preserve the perfs. Gum is typically hinged, sometimes heavily.

ONE CENT (No. 443). Frequently faked. Scrutinize line pairs carefully. Never hinged copies are not scarce. Premium unused are not difficult; premium line pairs are moderately difficult.

TWO CENT (No. 444). Frequently faked. Scrutinize line pairs carefully. Never hinged copies are not scarce. Premium unused are not difficult; genuine line pairs in premium condition are difficult.

THREE CENT (No. 445). Frequently faked, especially line pairs. Scrutinize line pairs carefully. Used copies are also frequently faked because of high catalogue value. Centering is better than on sheet stamps of the same issue. Never hinged copies are scarce. Premium unused pairs are difficult; premium line pairs are extremely difficult. Get a certificate on this one.

FOUR CENT (No. 446). Line pairs can be faked, but rarely are. Unused singles and pairs are sometimes faked, trimmed from sheet stock. Used fakes are more commonly encountered because of their relatively high catalogue value; genuine used copies are fairly scarce. Centering is better than on sheet stamps of the same issue. Never hinged copies are scarce. Premium unused singles and pairs are difficult; premium line pairs are extremely difficult.

FIVE CENT (No. 447). Unused copies are seldom faked. Because of their relatively high catalogue value, used stamps are frequently faked, trimmed from sheet stock. Centering is better than on sheet stamps of the same issue. Never hinged copies are not scarce. Premium unused singles and pairs are not difficult; premium line pairs are moderately difficult.

Premium Characteristics
Sound condition, balanced margins, fresh color, reasonably uniform perforations, never hinged, if unused; light cancel, if used.

Caveats
Beware fakes. Beware regumming. Certificate strongly recommended for line pairs, and more expensive singles and pairs, especially never hinged.

WASHINGTON-FRANKLIN COILS
Perf 10 Horizontally,
Single Line Watermark
SCOTT NOS. 449-50

Scarcity
Quantity Issued: not known

General Comments
These stamps are usually poorly centered. Spacing of rows of perfs can be inconsistent, sometimes crowding the top and bottom margins of pairs as seen on the right. Irregular perfs are characteristic of perf 10s, and not considered a fault. Pairs are occasionally seen clipped apart, retaining parts of adjoining stamps in order to preserve the perfs. Copies are typically hinged, sometimes heavily.

TWO CENT, Type I (No. 449). This is a very rare coil. Usually poorly centered. However, the illustrated example of No. 449 (on the left) is worse than usual. Copies often tend to be more evenly spaced between straight edges, as is the case with the pair of No. 450 (on the right). Rarely faked, but occasionally found altered from less expensive stamps with lines of shading scraped away. Premium unused pairs are extremely rare, as are never hinged pairs; line pairs are exceedingly rare in both categories.

TWO CENT, Type II (No. 450). Centering is not the best, but this coil is sufficiently abundant so that premium copies are easy to find. Never hinged copies are available. Line pairs, however, are much scarcer than generally known. The illustrated line pair on the right is a very nice example. Frequently faked. Scrutinize line pairs carefully.

Premium characteristics
Sound condition, balanced margins, fresh color, reasonably uniform perforations, never hinged (light hinge okay on Scott No. 449), if unused; light cancel, if used.

Caveats
Beware fakes. Beware regumming. Certificate absolutely essential for No. 449.

Natural inclusions (wood fibers, carbon specks, etc.) were inherent in the manufacture of paper used for certain issues such as the Columbians, Trans-Mississippis, Panama-Pacifics, and Washington-Franklins. They are especially noticeable on yellow, red and orange stamps. While aesthetically distracting, they should not be considered faults, *per se*.

WASHINGTON-FRANKLIN COILS
Rotary Press, Perf 10 Vertically,
Single Line Watermark
SCOTT NOS. 452-58

Scarcity
Quantity Issued: not known

General Comments
Centering is variable because the space between stamps is somewhat narrower than on flat plate printings; most copies are poorly centered. Spacing of rows of perfs can be inconsistent, as on the strip of four above (No. 454). The two illustrated pairs (No. 456) are nicely centered for this issue and much better than normal, especially the line pair. Irregular perfs are characteristic of perf 10s, and not considered a fault. Note the condition of perfs in the illustration. Pairs are occasionally seen clipped apart, retaining parts of adjoining stamps in order to preserve the perfs. Gum is typically hinged, sometimes heavily.

ONE CENT (No. 452). Never hinged copies are available. Pairs in premium condition are not especially difficult because of large population; premium line pairs are somewhat more difficult.
TWO CENT, Type I (No. 453). Never hinged copies are scarce. Pairs in premium condition are difficult; premium line pairs are very difficult.

TWO CENT, Type II (No. 454). Never hinged copies are scarce. Pairs in premium condition are difficult; premium line pairs are very difficult.
TWO CENT, Type III (No. 455). Never hinged copies are available. Pairs in premium condition are not difficult; premium line pairs are moderately difficult. Although not expensive, this stamp is sometimes faked, but not often enough to be a problem.
THREE CENT, Type I (No. 456). Never hinged copies are scarce. Pairs in premium condition are difficult; premium line pairs are extremely difficult.
FOUR CENT (No. 457). Never hinged copies are available. Pairs in premium condition are difficult; premium line pairs are very difficult.
FIVE CENT (No. 458). Never hinged copies are available. Pairs in premium condition are difficult; premium line pairs are very difficult.

Premium characteristics
Sound condition, balanced margins, fresh color, reasonably uniform perforations, never hinged, if unused; light cancel, if used.

Caveats
Beware regumming. Some fakes exist. Certificate recommended for line pairs and more expensive singles and pairs, especially never hinged.

**2c CARMINE, Imperforate
Single Line Watermark**
YEAR OF ISSUE: 1914
SCOTT NO. 459

Scarcity
Quantity Issued: not known
★ Average No./Auction: .75

Hinging
NH: 54.1%
Hinged: 45.9%

Comments
An imperforate, therefore, centering
not much of a problem. Gum is

typically hinged, often heavily, however, never
hinged copies are not scarce. Used examples
should have a contemporaneous cancel
(1914-1920), not a later or fake cancel.
Genuine used copies with contemporaneous
cancels are very rare. Regard used singles
as fakes, unless certified. Pairs are rarely
faked. Line pairs are usually faulty (creased);
line pairs without creases command a
premium.

Premium Characteristics
Sound condition, balanced margins, bright
color, never hinged, if unused; neat,
contemporaneous cancel, if used. Premium
unused copies are not terribly difficult, except
line pairs, which are often creased. Used
copies in any condition are rare.

Caveats
Beware faults and repairs, including
regumming. Certificate recommended for
unused, and is essential for used copies.

**$1 VIOLET BLACK, Perf 10,
Double Line Watermark**
YEAR OF ISSUE: 1915
SCOTT NO. 460

Scarcity
Quantity Issued: not known
★ Average No./Auction: .54

Hinging
NH: 15.1%
Hinged: 84.9%

General Comments
This stamp is notoriously poorly
centered. The illustrated examples
are better than normally encountered.
Irregular perfs are to be expected and

not considered a fault; that's just the way they
come. Note the condition of the perfs in the
illustration; they are perfectly acceptable.
Gum is usually hinged, often heavily, or
disturbed. Faults, frequently hinge thins, are
commonplace.
Used copies are usually heavily canceled and
atrociously centered. Regumming is frequent
enough to be a problem.

Premium Characteristics
Sound condition, balanced margins (jumbo
margined copies are worth a considerable
premium), bright color, reasonably uniform
perfs, never hinged or lightly, if unused.
Unused copies with all the premium elements
are exceedingly difficult; premium used
copies, although not expensive, are
surprisingly difficult.

Caveats
Beware faults and repairs, including
regumming and reperfing. Certificate
recommended, especially for never hinged.

2c PALE CARMINE RED, Perf 11
Single Line Watermark
YEAR OF ISSUE: 1915
SCOTT NO. 461

Scarcity
Quantity Issued: not known
★ Average No./Auction: .67

Hinging
NH: 47.0%
Hinged: 53.0%

Comments
Margins tend to be small; centering is variable, with many poorly centered. Frequently faked both unused and used. Used examples should have a contemporaneous cancel, not a later or fake cancel. Genuine used copies are very scarce. Never hinged copies are not scarce.

Premium Characteristics
Sound condition, balanced margins, bright color, never hinged, if unused. Premium copies are elusive.

Caveats
Beware fakes. Beware faults and repairs, including regumming. Certificate strongly recommended, especially for used.

WASHINGTON-FRANKLIN SERIES
Perf 10, Unwatermarked
SCOTT NOS. 462-80

Scarcity
Quantity Issued: not known

General Comments
This series is much scarcer than the watermarked issued (Scott Nos. 424-440). The absence of watermark must be carefully ascertained; frequently stamps offered as unwatermarked are actually from the previous watermarked issue. These stamps are notoriously poorly centered. Refer to page 127 for general comments about centering, perfs, gum, faults, etc. on perf 10s, and for illustrations. Used copies are usually heavily canceled and poorly centered; nice copies are irritatingly difficult.

ONE & TWO CENT (No. 462-3). Premium copies are not difficult.
THREE CENT (No. 464). Premium copies are moderately difficult.
FOUR & FIVE CENT (No. 465-6). Premium copies are difficult. No. 466 often faked from Scott No. 496.
SIX CENT (No. 468). Color subject to chemical change (browning). Premium copies are difficult, especially NH.
SEVEN CENT (No. 469). Premium copies are very difficult, especially never hinged.

EIGHT & NINE CENT (No. 470-1). Premium copies are difficult, especially NH.
TEN CENT (No. 472). Premium copies are very difficult, especially never hinged. Often faked from Scott No. 497.
ELEVEN CENT (No. 473). More common than other high values. Premium copies are difficult.
TWELVE CENT (No. 474). Premium copies are very difficult, especially never hinged.
FIFTEEN CENT (No. 475). Usually a pale, low contrast shade. Deep rich color is prized. Premium copies are extremely difficult, especially never hinged.
TWENTY CENT (No. 476). Premium copies are extremely difficult, especially NH.

Premium Characteristics
Sound condition, balanced margins (jumbo margined copies are worth a substantial premium), reasonably uniform perfs, fresh color, never hinged, if unused; light cancel, if used. Never hinged copies are easier to locate than nicely centered copies.

Caveats
Beware of stamps with barely noticeable watermarks. Check carefully to make sure watermark is definitely not present. Beware faults and repairs, including regumming and reperfing. Certificate recommended for never hinged on the more expensive values.

30c ORANGE RED, Perf 10, Unwatermarked
YEAR OF ISSUE: 1916 (?)
SCOTT NO. 476A

Scarcity
Quantity Issued: 200
★ Average No./Auction: .06

Comments
Two sheets reportedly known, one of which has been broken up for singles and blocks at this writing. Stamps from the broken sheet are all poorly centered to a greater or lesser degree, as illustrated in the photo. Most copies are never hinged. Used copies are not known.

Premium Characteristics
Sound condition, bright color, never hinged original gum.

Caveats
Certificate essential.

50c VIOLET, Perf 10, Unwatermarked
YEAR OF ISSUE: 1917
SCOTT NO. 477

Scarcity
Quantity Issued: not known
★ Average No./Auction: .77

Hinging
NH: 14.7%
Hinged: 85.3%

Comments
This stamp is the key to the set. It is typically poorly centered. Its violet color often appears light or faded.

Fresh, lustrously colored copies are scarce and command a premium. Refer to page 127 for general comments about centering, perfs, gum, faults, etc. on perf 10s. Centering and perfs on the illustrated example are characteristic. Gum is typically hinged, often heavily. Used copies are usually heavily canceled and atrociously centered.

Premium Characteristics
Sound condition, balanced margins (jumbo margined copies are worth a considerable premium), bright color, reasonably uniform perfs, never hinged or lightly hinged original gum, if unused. Premium unused copies are exceedingly difficult, especially never hinged. Premium used copies, although not expensive, are surprisingly difficult.

Caveats
Beware faults and repairs, including regumming and reperfing. Certificate strongly recommended, and essential for never hinged.

$1 VIOLET BROWN, Perf 10, Unwatermarked
YEAR OF ISSUE: 1916
SCOTT NO. 478

Scarcity
Quantity Issued: not known
★ Average No./Auction: .79

Hinging
NH: 19.2%
Hinged: 80.8%

Comments
Refer to page 127 for general

comments about centering, perfs, gum, faults, etc. on perf 10s. Centering and perfs on the illustrated example are characteristic. Gum is typically hinged, often heavily. Used copies are usually heavily canceled and atrociously centered.

Premium Characteristics
Sound condition, balanced margins (jumbo margined copies are worth a considerable premium), bright color, reasonably uniform perfs, never hinged or lightly hinged original gum, if unused. Premium unused copies are exceedingly difficult, especially never hinged. Premium used copies, although not expensive, are surprisingly difficult.

Caveats
Beware faults and repairs, including regumming and reperfing. Certificate strongly recommended, especially for never hinged.

$2 DARK BLUE, Perf 10, Unwatermarked
YEAR OF ISSUE: 1917
SCOTT NO. 479

Scarcity
Quantity Issued: 305,380
★ Average No./Auction: 1.02

Hinging
NH: 28.7%
Hinged: 71.3%

Comments
Refer to page 127 for general comments about centering, perfs,

gum, faults, etc. on perf 10s. Centering and perfs on the illustrated example are characteristic. Gum is typically hinged, often heavily, however, never hinged copies are not as scarce as for Nos. 477-78. Nevertheless, finding *premium* never hinged copies is a challenge. Used copies are usually heavily canceled and atrociously centered.

Premium Characteristics
Sound condition, balanced margins (jumbo margined copies are worth a considerable premium), bright color, reasonably uniform perfs, never hinged original gum, if unused. Premium unused copies are exceedingly difficult, especially never hinged. Premium used copies, although not expensive, are surprisingly difficult.

Caveats
Beware faults and repairs, including regumming and reperfing. Certificate strongly recommended, especially for never hinged.

$5 LIGHT GREEN, Perf 10, Unwatermarked
YEAR OF ISSUE: 1917
SCOTT NO. 480

Scarcity
Quantity Issued: 217,167
★ Average No./Auction: 1.40

Hinging
NH: 29.5%
Hinged: 70.5%

Comments
Refer to page 127 for general comments about centering, perfs, gum, faults, etc. on perf 10s. Centering and perfs on the illustrated example are characteristic. Gum is typically hinged, often heavily, however, never hinged copies are not as scarce as for Nos. 477-78. Nevertheless, finding *premium* never hinged copies is a challenge. Used copies are usually heavily canceled and atrociously centered.

Premium Characteristics
Sound condition, balanced margins (jumbo margined copies are worth a considerable premium), bright color, reasonably uniform perfs, never hinged original gum, if unused. Premium unused copies are exceedingly difficult, especially never hinged. Premium used copies, although not expensive, are surprisingly difficult.

Caveats
Beware faults and repairs, including regumming and reperfing. Certificate strongly recommended, especially for never hinged.

5c CARMINE ERROR
Perf 10, Unwatermarked
SCOTT NO. 467

Scarcity
Quantity Issued: not known
★ Avg. No./Auction (block of 9): .11
★ Avg. No./Auction (block of 12): .15

Comments
This error is usually collected in blocks of nine or twelve, containing either one or two error stamps, respectively, in the center of the block. The blocks are notoriously poorly centered. The illustrated example is quite acceptable. Blocks are typically hinged at the top, and sometimes at the bottom; the error stamps themselves are usually never hinged. Copies are known postally used, but are rare.

Premium Characteristics
Blocks, free of perforation separations, with reasonable centering, fresh color, lightly hinged or never hinged, if unused.

Caveats
Beware faults and repairs. Beware separated perforations. Certificate recommended for never hinged, essential for used stamp on cover.

2c DEEP ROSE, Imperforate
Unwatermarked
YEAR OF ISSUE: 1920
SCOTT NO. 482A

Scarcity
Quantity Issued: not known, rare
★ Average No./Auction: .00
☉ Average No./Auction: .02

Comments
A very rare stamp. Imperforate, only known used (all singles, except for one pair) and then with oblong Schermack Type III private perfs. Very scarce with the perf bars clear of the design. The perf bars are often clipped off on one side. Fakes exist.

Premium Characteristics
This stamp is very difficult to locate in any condition. Its rarity does not permit selectivity in the normal sense.

Caveats
Beware fakes. Certificate essential.

5c CARMINE ERROR
Imperforate, Unwatermarked
SCOTT NO. 485

Scarcity
Quantity Issued: 50 blocks of nine; 50 blocks of twelve
★ Avg. No./Auction (block of 9): .01
★ Avg. No./Auction (block of 12): .01

Comments
A very rare stamp. This is the same stamp as No. 467, except imperforate. Like No. 467, it is collected in blocks of nine or twelve, containing either one or two error stamps, respectively, in the center of the block. Being imperforate, centering is generally not a problem.

The blocks are typically hinged at the top, and sometimes at the bottom; the error stamps themselves are usually never hinged. Paper inclusions are often encountered on this issue. Never hinged blocks are exceedingly rare. Not known used.

Premium Characteristics
Free of faults, fresh color, lightly hinged or never hinged.

Caveats
Beware faults and repairs. Certificate recommended for gum, especially never hinged.

WASHINGTON-FRANKLIN COILS
Rotary Press, Perf 10 Horizontally
Unwatermarked
SCOTT NOS. 486-89

Scarcity
Quantity Issued: not known

Comments
These coils share the same characteristics as other perf 10 coils.

Premium characteristics
Sound condition, balanced margins, fresh color, reasonably uniform perfs, never hinged, if unused; light cancel, if used. These coils are abundant; locating premium copies is not difficult.

Caveats
Beware Type III stamps with lines of shading scraped away to resemble Scott No. 487. Scrutinize line pairs.

WASHINGTON-FRANKLIN COILS
Rotary Press, Perf 10 Vertically,
Unwatermarked
SCOTT NOS. 491-97

Scarcity
Quantity Issued: not known

General Comments
Usually poorly centered. Spacing of rows
of perfs can be inconsistent (refer to the
illustration on page 131). Irregular perfs
are characteristic of perf 10s, and not
considered a fault. Pairs are occasionally
seen clipped apart, retaining parts of
adjoining stamps in order to preserve the
perfs. Gum is typically hinged, often
heavily, however, never hinged copies
are not scarce. Fakes are not generally a
problem, however, check line pairs
carefully.

ONE CENT (No. 490). Abundant. Never
hinged and premium copies no problem.
TWO CENT, Type II (No. 491). See below.
TWO CENT, Type III (No. 492). Relatively
abundant. Never hinged available.
Premium copies no problem.
THREE CENT, Type I (No. 493). Relatively
abundant. Never hinged available.
Premium pairs no problem; premium line
pairs more difficult.
THREE CENT, Type II (No. 494). Relatively
abundant. Never hinged available.
Premium pairs no problem; premium line
pairs more difficult.
FOUR CENT (No. 495). Relatively abundant.
Never hinged available. Premium pairs
no problem; premium line pairs more
difficult.
FIVE CENT (No. 496). Relatively abundant.
Never hinged available. Premium pairs
no problem; premium line pairs more
difficult.
TEN CENT (No. 497). Relatively abundant.
Never hinged available. Premium pairs
not difficult; premium line pairs very
scarce.

Premium characteristics
Sound condition, balanced margins, fresh
color, reasonably uniform perfs, never
hinged, if unused; light cancel, if used.

Caveats
Beware regumming. Check line pairs.
Certificate recommended for more
expensive never hinged line pairs.

WASHINGTON-FRANKLIN COIL
Rotary Press, Perf 10 Vertically
Unwatermarked
SCOTT NO. 491

Scarcity
Quantity Issued: very rare

Comments
A very rare coil. Shares the same
characteristics as other rotary press, perf
10 coils, however a fair number of copies
are reasonably centered as in the
illustration. Seldom faked, however,
sometimes fakes are encountered from
Type III stamps with lines of shading in
the ribbons scraped away to resemble
Type II. Never hinged copies very rare.
Line pairs are extremely rare. Used
copies are also rare, especially pairs.

Premium characteristics
Sound condition, reasonably balanced
margins, bold color, lightly hinged or
never hinged (NH is very tough), if
unused. Premium unused copies are
difficult.

Caveats
Beware fakes. Certificate essential.

CAUTION: Used copies of many imperfs and coil stamps (such as Scott Nos. 315, 459, 491, 539, 578,
579, 595, etc.) are very scarce. Fake cancels are sometimes applied to no-gum unused examples to
make them more "salable." Be cautious of cancels on rare stamps whose value used is as much as
or more than unused.

WASHINGTON-FRANKLIN SERIES
Perf 11, Unwatermarked
SCOTT NOS. 498-518

Scarcity
Quantity Issued: not known

General Comments
Perforations separate much more cleanly on perf 11s than on perf 10s, therefore, irregular perfs are not as much a problem. Note the condition of the perfs in the illustration. Although usually poorly centered, this issue is more abundant than previous Washington-Franklins, therefore, finding nice copies is not nearly so difficult. The illustrated examples are all nicely margined gems. Gum is typically hinged, often heavily, however, never hinged copies are more abundant than for previous issues. Used copies are usually heavily canceled and poorly centered, making premium copies, although inexpensive, irritatingly difficult.

ONE CENT (No. 498). Premium copies are not difficult.
TWO CENT, Type I (No. 499). Premium copies are not difficult.
TWO CENT, Type Ia (No. 500). A very scarce stamp. Sound more often than not, and often never hinged. Nevertheless, well centered, premium copies are elusive.
THREE CENT, Type I (No. 501). Premium copies are difficult.
THREE CENT, Type II (No. 502). Premium copies are difficult.
FOUR CENT (No. 503). Premium copies are not difficult.
FIVE CENT (No. 504). Premium copies are not difficult.
FIVE CENT ERROR (No. 505). Separate listing follows this section.
SIX CENT (No. 506). Color subject to chemical change (browning). Premium copies are difficult.
SEVEN CENT (No. 507). Premium copies are somewhat difficult.
EIGHT CENT (No. 508). Premium copies are somewhat difficult.
NINE CENT (No. 509). Premium copies are somewhat difficult.
TEN CENT (No. 510). Premium copies are somewhat difficult.
ELEVEN CENT (No. 511). More abundant than other high values. Premium copies are not difficult.
TWELVE CENT (No. 512). Premium copies are somewhat difficult.
THIRTEEN CENT (No. 513). Exists in numerous shades. Premium copies are not difficult.
FIFTEEN CENT (No. 514). Premium copies are difficult.
TWENTY CENT (No. 515). Premium copies are difficult.
THIRTY CENT (No. 516). Premium copies are not difficult.
FIFTY CENT (No. 517). Premium copies are difficult.
ONE DOLLAR VIOLET BROWN (No. 518). Premium copies are difficult.
ONE DOLLAR DEEP BROWN (No. 518b). Separate listing follows.

Premium Characteristics
Sound condition, balanced margins (jumbo margined copies are prized and worth a substantial premium), fresh color, never hinged, if unused; light cancel, if used.

Caveats
Beware faults and repairs, including regumming and reperfing. Certificate recommended for never hinged premium copies of the more expensive values.

$1 DEEP BROWN
Perf 11, Unwatermarked
YEAR OF ISSUE: 1917
SCOTT NO. 518b

Scarcity
Quantity Issued: rare
★ Average No./Auction: .05
⊚ Average No./Auction: .01

Comments
This stamp is rare and seldom encountered. It is typically poorly centered, and often tightly margined. The illustrated example is about as nice as they come. Many are faulty. Gum is usually hinged, often heavily. Never hinged copies are very scarce.

Premium Characteristics
The population of this stamp is too small to permit selectivity in the normal sense.

Caveats
Beware faults and repairs, including regumming and reperfing. Certificate essential.

5c CARMINE ERROR
Perf 11, Unwatermarked
SCOTT NO. 505

Scarcity
Quantity Issued: not known
★ Avg. No./Auction (block of 9): .42
★ Avg. No./Auction (block of 12): .23

Comments
This error is same error as Nos. 467 and 485. It is usually collected in blocks of nine or twelve, containing either one or two error stamps respectively, in the center of the block. Singles and strips of three with the error stamp at center are also known. Blocks are notoriously poorly centered. Centering on the illustrated example is typical for the issue; better and worse examples also exist. Blocks are often hinged at the top, and sometimes at the bottom; the error stamps themselves are usually never hinged. Postally used singles are rare.

Premium Characteristics
Sound condition, reasonable centering, fresh color, lightly hinged or never hinged; blocks should be free of perf separations.

Caveats
Beware faults and repairs. Beware separated perforations on blocks. Certificate recommended for never hinged, and is essential for used stamp on cover.

2c CARMINE, Perf 11
Double Line Watermarked
YEAR OF ISSUE: 1917
SCOTT NO. 519

Scarcity
Quantity Issued: not known, scarce
★ Average No./Auction: .52
⊚ Average No./Auction: .06

Comments
While often poorly centered, this stamp is not as difficult in premium condition as other Washington-Franklins. The illustrated example is a beauty. Although this stamp is scarce, many are never hinged. Regumming is encountered occasionally. It is very scarce used with contemporaneous cancel. No top plate blocks are known, only bottom and side. This stamp is frequently faked, especially used. Refer to the cautionary note at the bottom of page 138.

Premium Characteristics
Sound condition, balanced margins, fresh color, never hinged, if unused; light cancel, if used.

Caveats
Beware fakes, especially used. Certificate essential.

$2 ORANGE RED & BLACK
YEAR OF ISSUE: 1918
SCOTT NO. 523

Scarcity
Quantity Issued: not known
★ Average No./Auction: 1.60
⊚ Average No./Auction: .23

Hinging
NH: 21.5%
Hinged: 78.5%

Comments
This stamp is routinely poorly centered. Copies with balanced margins are very difficult; the illustrated examples are typical of the issue, and better than many. Used copies are often heavily canceled. Gum is usually hinged, often heavily.

Premium Characteristics
Sound condition, balanced margins (jumbo margined copies are worth a substantial premium), fresh color, lightly hinged or never hinged, if unused; light cancel, if used. Both premium unused and used copies are very difficult.

Caveats
Beware faults and repairs, including regumming and reperfing. Certificate recommended for premium copies, especially never hinged.

$5 DEEP GREEN & BLACK
YEAR OF ISSUE: 1918
SCOTT NO. 524

Scarcity
Quantity Issued: 296,653
★ Average No./Auction: 2.00

Hinging
NH: 41.9%
Hinged: 58.1%

Comments
This stamp is typically poorly centered. Copies with balanced margins are difficult, as the illustration reveals. The example on the far left is gem. Gum is usually hinged, often heavily. Never hinged copies are scarcer than the auction statistic suggests. Used copies are often heavily canceled.

Premium Characteristics
Sound condition, balanced margins (jumbo margined copies are worth a considerable premium), fresh color, lightly hinged or never hinged, if unused; light cancel, if used. Premium unused copies are very difficult. Premium used copies, although relatively inexpensive, are also difficult.

Caveats
Beware faults and repairs, including regumming and reperfing. Certificate recommended for premium condition, especially never hinged.

2c CARMINE, Type V
Offset, Imperforate
YEAR OF ISSUE: 1920
SCOTT NO. 533

Scarcity
Quantity Issued: not known
★ Average No./Auction: .36

Hinging
NH: 47.2%
Hinged: 52.8%

Comments
Being imperforate, this stamp is usually well centered. Gum is typically hinged, sometimes heavily, however, never hinged copies are not scarce. Fakes exist, especially used singles created by trimming perforated copies. Except for margin singles with abundant selvedge, singles should be regarded with suspicion unless certified.

Premium Characteristics
Sound condition, balanced margins, fresh color, never hinged, if unused; light cancel, if used. Both premium unused and used copies are elusive.

Caveats
Beware fakes. Beware faults and repairs, including regumming. Certificate recommended, essential for single copies.

12274

2c CARMINE, Type VII
Offset, Imperforate
YEAR OF ISSUE: 1920
SCOTT NO. 534B

Scarcity
Quantity Issued: not known, rare
★ Average No./Auction: .21
◉ Average No./Auction: .06

Hinging
NH: 33.3%
Hinged: 66.7%

Comments
This stamp is very scarce. Check for clear, discernable Type VII characteristics. Being imperforate, centering is not usually a problem. Gum is typically hinged, often heavily. Never hinged copies are scarcer than the auction statistic suggests. Fakes exist, especially used singles, created by trimming perforated copies. Except for margin singles with abundant selvedge, singles should be regarded with extreme suspicion unless certified. The illustrated example is a gem top margin plate single.

Premium Characteristics
Sound condition, balanced margins, fresh color, never hinged, if unused; light cancel, if used. Premium unused copies are somewhat difficult.

Caveats
Beware fakes. Beware faults and repairs, including regumming. Certificate recommended for all copies.

2c CARMINE ROSE, Perf 11x10
YEAR OF ISSUE: 1919
SCOTT NO. 539

Scarcity
Quantity Issued: not known
★ Average No./Auction: .20
◉ Average No./Auction: .01

Hinging
NH: 16.0%
Hinged: 84.0%

Comments
This stamp is very rare, possesses a

characteristic dull, fuzzy appearance, and is notoriously small margined and poorly centered. The illustrated example is typical; anything better is a bonus. Gum is usually hinged, sometimes heavily. Used copies are rare. Fakes exist, usually from Type III stamps with lines of shading scraped away to resemble Type II. Refer to the cautionary note at the bottom of page 138.

Premium Characteristics
Sound condition, reasonable centering (within the limits of the issue), fresh color, lightly hinged or never hinged, if unused; light cancel, if used. This stamp is very difficult in any condition; do not have unreasonably high expectations about quality.

Caveats
Beware fakes. Beware faults and repairs, including regumming and reperfing. Certificate essential.

1c GREEN, Perf 11
YEAR OF ISSUE: 1923
SCOTT NO. 544

Scarcity
Quantity Issued: very rare
★ Average No./Auction: .04
⊙ Average No./Auction: .12

Comments
A very rare stamp. It is notoriously poorly centered, especially unused. Unused copies are usually centered to top right. Consider any centering better than that of the illustrated example a bonus. Used copies may have either a precancel or regular cancel. A fair number of never hinged copies exist due to a find in the 1970s (two of the four copies that appeared at auction in the survey were never hinged).

Premium Characteristics
An extremely limited population does not permit selectivity in the normal sense.

Caveats
Certificate essential.

1c GREEN, Perf 11
YEAR OF ISSUE: 1921
SCOTT NO. 545

Scarcity
Quantity Issued: not known
★ Average No./Auction: .21
⊙ Average No./Auction: .05

Hinging
NH: 33.3%
Hinged: 66.7%

Comments
This stamp is somewhat small margined and typically poorly centered. The illustrated example is better than often encountered. Gum is usually hinged, sometimes heavily. Never hinged copies are not terribly scarce, however, nicely centered never hinged copies are tough. Used copies are scarce. Refer to the cautionary note at the bottom of page 138.

Premium Characteristics
Sound condition, reasonable centering, fresh color, never hinged, if unused; light cancel, if used. Premium copies are extremely difficult.

Caveats
Beware faults and repairs, including regumming and reperfing. Certificate strongly recommended.

2c CARMINE ROSE, Perf 11
YEAR OF ISSUE: 1921
SCOTT NO. 546

Scarcity
Quantity Issued: not known
★ Average No./Auction: .38
⊙ Average No./Auction: .04

Hinging
NH: 74.1%
Hinged: 25.9%

Comments
This stamp is small margined and notoriously poorly centered. The illustrated example is beautifully centered but shows characteristically small margins. Color is typically strong and vivid. Never hinged copies are relatively abundant. Nicely centered copies are much more difficult to find than never hinged copies. Watch out for regumming.

Premium Characteristics
Sound condition, reasonably balanced margins, vivid color, never hinged, if unused; light cancel, if used. Premium copies are extremely difficult, especially well centered.

Caveats
Beware faults and repairs, including reperfing and regumming. Certificate recommended.

$2 CARMINE & BLACK
YEAR OF ISSUE: 1920
SCOTT NO. 547

Scarcity
Quantity Issued: not known
★ Average No./Auction: 2.18

Hinging
NH: 43.8%
Hinged: 56.2%

Comments
This stamp is typically poorly centered. However, it is much more abundant than its orange-red and black counterpart (No. 523) and therefore not as difficult to locate in premium condition. Also, its margins tend to be larger than those on lower denomination Washington-Franklins. The illustrated examples on the left possess reasonably balanced margins; those on the right are more typically centered. Copies with reasonably balanced margins are moderately difficult; copies with perfectly balanced margins are extremely elusive, especially never hinged. A relatively large number of never hinged copies exist, however, hinged copies are often heavily so. Used copies are usually heavily canceled.

Premium Characteristics
Sound condition, balanced margins (jumbo margined copies command a premium), fresh color, never hinged, if unused; light cancel, if used. Both premium unused and used copies are moderately difficult.

Caveats
Beware faults and repairs, including regumming and reperfing. Certificate recommended for premium copies, especially for never hinged.

DEFINITIVE SERIES OF 1922-25
Flat Plate Printing, Perf 11
SCOTT NOS. 551-71

Scarcity
Quantity Issued: not known

General Comments
Stamps of this series are small margined and usually poorly centered, but nowhere near as difficult as the Washington-Franklins. The illustrated examples are gems; especially the 7-cent, whose margins are enormous for this issue. The 11-cent exists in a interesting variety of shades, which are popular with specialists; the deeper being more appealing to the general collector. Gum, is typically hinged, often heavily, nevertheless, ample quantities of never hinged copies exist; they are not scarce. Natural gum skips occasionally occur. Repairs, including regumming and reperfing, are not widespread, however, it is prudent to examine the more expensive values carefully.

Premium Characteristics
Sound condition, balanced margins (jumbo margined copies are worth a premium), fresh, rich color, never hinged, if unused; light cancel, if used. Premium copies are not terribly difficult.

Caveats
Beware regumming and reperfing. Certificate recommended for the more expensive never hinged premium copies.

$2 DEEP BLUE
YEAR OF ISSUE: 1923
SCOTT NO. 572

Scarcity
Quantity Issued: 2,950,000 est.
★ Average No./Auction: 1.27

Hinging
NH: 69.0%
Hinged: 31.0%

Comments
This stamp is not difficult to find well centered. The illustrated example shows typical margin size. Many copies are hinged, however, never hinged copies are relatively abundant. Natural gum skips occasionally occur. Regumming is sometimes encountered, but only infrequently.

Premium Characteristics
Sound condition, balanced margins (jumbo margined copies exist), fresh color, never hinged, if unused. Premium copies are not difficult.

Caveats
Beware faults and repairs, including regumming. Certificate not necessary unless buyer is inexperienced recognizing original gum.

$5 CARMINE & BLUE
YEAR OF ISSUE: 1923
SCOTT NO. 573

Scarcity
Quantity Issued: 1,250,000 est.
★ Average No./Auction: 2.40

Hinging
NH: 69.5%
Hinged: 30.5%

Comments
This stamp is not difficult to find well centered. The illustrated example shows typical margin size. Many copies are hinged, however, never hinged copies are relatively abundant. Natural gum skips occasionally occur. Regumming is sometimes encountered, but only infrequently.

Premium Characteristics
Sound condition, balanced margins (jumbo margined copies exist), fresh colors, never hinged, if unused. Premium copies are not difficult.

Caveats
Beware faults and repairs, including regumming. Certificate not necessary unless buyer is inexperienced recognizing original gum.

1c GREEN, Perf 11x10
YEAR OF ISSUE: 1923
SCOTT NO. 578

Scarcity
Quantity Issued: not known
★ Average No./Auction: .51

Hinging
NH: 80.0%
Hinged: 20.0%

Comments
This stamp is small margined and typically poorly centered. Irregular perfs are commonplace, especially on the perf 10 side, and not considered a fault. The illustrated example is very nicely centered and margined for this issue. Never hinged copies are abundant. Fakes exist. Refer to the cautionary note at the bottom of page 138.

Premium Characteristics
Sound condition, reasonably balanced margins, fresh color, never hinged, if unused; light cancel, if used. Nicely centered copies are difficult.

Caveats
Beware fakes. Beware faults and repairs, including regumming and reperfing. Certificate recommended.

2c CARMINE, Perf 11x10
YEAR OF ISSUE: 1923
SCOTT NO. 579

Scarcity
Quantity Issued: not known
★ Average No./Auction: .54

Hinging
NH: 66.0%
Hinged: 34.0%

Comments
This stamp is small margined and typically poorly centered. Irregular perfs are commonplace, especially on the perf 10 side, and not considered a fault. The illustrated example is very nicely centered and margined for this issue. Never hinged copies are abundant. Fakes exist but are encountered only infrequently. Refer to the cautionary note at the bottom of page 138.

Premium Characteristics
Sound condition, reasonably balanced margins, fresh color, never hinged, if unused; light cancel, if used. Nicely centered copies are difficult.

Caveats
Beware faults and repairs, including regumming and reperfing. Certificate recommended.

DEFINITIVE SERIES OF 1923-26
Rotary Press Printing, Perf 10
SCOTT NOS. 581-91

Scarcity
Quantity Issued: not known

General Comments
Centering is notoriously poor as the illustrated blocks—which are typical for this issue—reveal. Side-to-side spacing between stamps is much narrower than top-to-bottom spacing. Nicely centered copies are very difficult. Irregular perfs are standard and not considered a fault. The spacing of the holes and the way these stamps separate, leaves perf tips looking uniformly short, as can be seen in the illustration.
Gum is typically hinged, however, never hinged copies are not scarce. It is—by

far—much easier to locate never hinged copies than nicely centered ones.
Some values are occasionally faked by reperfing perf 10 coils of the same designs. Used copies are usually heavily canceled and poorly centered, making premium copies irritatingly difficult.

Premium Characteristics
Sound condition, reasonable centering (within the limits of the issue), fresh color, never hinged, if unused; light cancel, if used. Nicely centered copies are tough.

Caveats
Beware fakes made from coils. Regumming seldom encountered, but the potential exists, so examine carefully. Certificate recommended only for never hinged premium copies of the more expensive values.

1c GREEN, Perf 11, Coil Waste
YEAR OF ISSUE: 1923
SCOTT NO. 594

Scarcity
Quantity Issued: very rare
★ Average No./Auction: .03
⊚ Average No./Auction: .06

Hinging
NH: 0.0%
Hinged:100.0%

Comments
This stamp is extremely rare, especially unused, and poorly centered, with perfs touching or cutting. The illustrated example is typical. Gum is notoriously poor: usually only partial original gum, disturbed gum, heavily hinged, or no gum. Lightly hinged copies should be considered premium. Never hinged copies, if they exist, are exceedingly rare (none were encountered in the auction survey).

Premium Characteristics
The rarity of this stamp does not permit selectivity in the normal sense.

Caveats
Certificate essential.

2c CARMINE, Perf 11, Coil Waste
YEAR OF ISSUE: 1923
SCOTT NO. 595

Scarcity
Quantity Issued: not known, scarce
★ Average No./Auction: .78
⊚ Average No./Auction: .06

Hinging
NH: 48.1%
Hinged: 51.9%

Comments
This stamp is small margined and notoriously poorly centered. The illustrated example is a gem, an uncommonly select copy. Never hinged copies are not scarce; in fact, never hinged copies are much easier to locate than nicely centered ones. Genuinely used copies are very scarce. Refer to the cautionary note at the bottom of page 138.

Premium Characteristics
Sound condition, reasonably balanced margins, fresh color, never hinged, if unused; light cancel, if used. Nicely centered, never hinged copies are difficult.

Caveats
Beware fake cancels. Certificate strongly recommended.

1c GREEN, Perf 11, Coil Waste
YEAR OF ISSUE: 1923
SCOTT NO. 596

Scarcity
Quantity Issued: very rare
★ Average No./Auction: .00
⊙ Average No./Auction: .01

Comments
A great rarity that seldom appears at auction. This stamp is notoriously poorly centered. The illustrated example displays typical centering. Not known unused. Usually precanceled KANSAS CITY, MO. Often with faults.

Premium Characteristics
The extreme rarity of this stamp does not permit selectivity in the normal sense.

Caveats
Certificate essential.

2c BLACK HARDING, Perf 11
YEAR OF ISSUE: 1923
SCOTT NO. 613

Scarcity
Quantity Issued: very rare
★ Average No./Auction: .00
⊙ Average No./Auction: .03

Comments
A great rarity that seldom appears at auction. This stamp is notoriously poorly centered. The illustrated example displays typical centering. It is not known unused. Often faulty or defective.

Premium Characteristics
The extreme rarity of this stamp does not permit selectivity in the normal sense.

Caveats
Certificate essential.

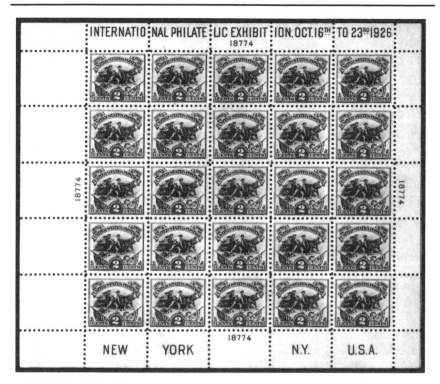

2c WHITE PLAINS SOUVENIR SHEET
YEAR OF ISSUE: 1926
SCOTT NO. 630

Scarcity
Quantity Issued: 107,398
★ Average No./Auction: 2.43

Hinging
NH: 58.9%
Hinged: 41.1%

Comments
Centering characteristically varies from one part of a sheet to another as can be seen on the illustrated example, which is typical and considered very fine for this issue. Some sheets are nicely centered throughout, but they few and far between. Knowledgeable buyers avoid sheets with perf separations. Sheets usually contain natural gum bends, and occasionally natural gum skips, which are not considered faults. However, sheets with severe gum creasing should be avoided. Never hinged copies are abundant. Used sheets are typically cancelled with first day cancels; those with non-first-day cancels are quite scarce.

Premium Characteristics
Sound condition, reasonable centering, fresh color, no perf separations, never hinged, if unused; neat, reasonable cancel, if used. Sheets possessing a high degree of perfection (fresh, never hinged, very well centered, no separations) are scarce and are worth a considerable premium. On the other hand, reasonably attractive (but not gem) sheets are not too difficult.

Caveats
Avoid sheets with weak perforations. Avoid toned sheets.

KANSAS-NEBRASKA OVERPRINT SET
YEAR OF ISSUE: 1928
SCOTT NOS. 658-68 & 669-79

Scarcity
Kansas Set, Quantities Issued:

No. 658	(1c)	13,390,000
No. 659	(1½c)	8,240,000
No. 660	(2c)	87,410,000
No. 661	(3c)	2,540,000
No. 662	(4c)	2,290,000
No. 663	(5c)	2,700,000
No. 664	(6c)	1,450,000
No. 665	(7c)	1,320,000
No. 666	(8c)	1,530,000
No. 667	(9c)	1,130,000
No. 668	(10c)	2,860,000

Nebraska Set, Quantities Issued:

No. 658	(1c)	8,220,000
No. 659	(1½c)	8,990,000
No. 660	(2c)	73,220,000
No. 661	(3c)	2,110,000
No. 662	(4c)	1,600,000
No. 663	(5c)	1,860,000
No. 664	(6c)	980,000
No. 665	(7c)	850,000
No. 666	(8c)	1,480,000
No. 667	(9c)	530,000
No. 668	(10c)	1,890,000

★ Avg No./Auction (Kans): .90
★ Avg No./Auction (Nebr): .74

Hinging (Kansas set)
NH: 42.7%
Hinged: 57.3%

Hinging (Nebraska set)
NH: 43.1%
Hinged: 56.9%

General Comments
These stamps are small margined and notoriously poorly centered. The illustrated blocks give an idea of centering typical of all stamps in the series. Note the narrow side-to-side spacing between stamps. Copies with balanced margins are extremely difficult; it is almost impossible to find complete sets with very fine centering throughout. Irregular perfs are commonplace and not considered a fault. Gum is typically hinged. Although never hinged copies are not scarce, they are more difficult than the same stamps without overprints. Never hinged copies are much easier to locate than nicely centered copies. Used copies are often faked, usually poorly, and often on the wrong stamp (genuine copies are always perforated 11x10½). Many fake overprints are typed or rubber stamped and obvious when compared to genuine examples. Unused fakes exist, but are not as frequently encountered.

Premium Characteristics
Sound condition, reasonable centering, fresh color, never hinged, if unused; light cancel, if used.

Caveats
Beware fakes, especially used stamps. Regumming is seldom encountered, but the potential exists, so examine purchases carefully.

$1 PURPLE & BLACK
Watermarked USIR
YEAR OF ISSUE: 1951
SCOTT NO. 832b

Scarcity
Quantity Issued: not known
★ Average No./Auction: .11
⊚ Average No./Auction: .09

Hinging
NH: 72.7%
Hinged: 27.3%

Comments
This stamp is more elusive than its price indicates. If demand were even moderately stronger, it would trade at a substantially higher price. It is usually well centered. Poorly centered copies are the exception. Most copies are never hinged. There is really not much of a premium for very fine copies, rather, poorly centered or hinged copies sell at a discount.

Premium Characteristics
Sound condition, balanced margins, fresh color, never hinged (without gum skips), if unused; light cancel, if used. Premium copies are not difficult

Caveats
Certificate recommended for unused.

$5 CARMINE & BLACK
YEAR OF ISSUE: 1938
SCOTT NO. 834

Scarcity
Quantity Issued: not known
★ Average No./Auction: 1.24

Hinging
NH: 91.1%
Hinged: 8.9%

Comments
This stamp is usually well centered. Poorly centered copies are the exception. Most copies are never hinged. Some copies possess natural gum skips. There is really no premium for very fine copies, rather, poorly centered copies and hinged copies sell at a discount. Regumming is seldom encountered.

Premium Characteristics
Sound condition, balanced margins, fresh color, never hinged (without gum skips), if unused; light cancel, if used. Premium copies are abundant.

Caveats
Certificate not necessary.

$5 RED BROWN & BLACK
SCOTT NO. 834a

Scarcity
Quantity Issued: not known
★ Average No./Auction: .04

Comments
A very rare stamp. Too few copies appeared at auction to yield a statistically valid result, but of the four

copies surveyed, two were never hinged. Often poorly centered, however, most copies are sound. Exceedingly rare used (none encountered in the auction survey).

Premium Characteristics
Population to small to permit selectivity.

Caveats
Certificate essential.

$5 BLACK
YEAR OF ISSUE: 1956
SCOTT NO. 1053

Scarcity
Quantity Issued: not known
★ Average No./Auction: .98

Hinging
NH: 77.3%
Hinged: 22.7%

Comments
Well centered copies are abundant, as are never hinged copies. There is really no premium for very fine copies (since that's the way most come), rather, poorly centered copies and hinged copies sell at a discount. This illustrated example is jumbo margined gem. Regumming is seldom encountered.

Premium Characteristics
Sound condition, balanced margins, fresh color, never hinged, if unused; light cancel, if used. Premium copies are abundant.

Caveats
Certificate not necessary.

6c ORANGE
YEAR OF ISSUE: 1918
SCOTT NO. C1

Scarcity
Quantity Issued: 2,134,988
★ Average No./Auction: 1.48

Hinging
NH: 67.3%
Hinged: 32.7%

Comments
Although not narrow margined, this stamp is typically poorly centered. Refer to the illustrations with No. C3 for an idea of the range of centering

to be expected on this series. No. C1 is susceptible to chemical change (browning). Freshly colored copies are desirable. Nicely centered copies with large margins are prized, and difficult, especially never hinged. This stamp is often hinged, however, never hinged copies are not scarce. Most copies appearing at auction were never hinged. Natural gum skips are occasionally encountered and not considered a fault. Refer to the note on page 117 regarding natural inclusions.

Premium Characteristics
Sound condition, balanced margins (jumbo margined copies are worth a substantial premium), fresh, bright color, never hinged (without gum skips), if unused; light cancel, if used. Copies possessing all the above premium attributes are very difficult.

Caveats
Beware regumming and reperfing. Certificate optional.

16c GREEN
YEAR OF ISSUE: 1918
SCOTT NO. C2

Scarcity
Quantity Issued: 3,793,987
★ Average No./Auction: 1.24

Hinging
NH: 70.5%
Hinged: 29.5%

Comments
Although not narrow margined, this stamp is typically poorly centered. Nicely centered copies with large margins are prized, and difficult, especially never hinged. Refer to the illustrations for No. C3 for an idea of the range of centering common to this issue. This stamp is often hinged, however, never hinged copies are not scarce. Most copies appearing at auction were never hinged. Natural gum skips are occasionally encountered and not considered a fault. Refer to the note on page 117 regarding natural inclusions.

Premium Characteristics
Sound condition, balanced margins (jumbo margined copies are worth a substantial premium), fresh color, never hinged (without gum skips), if unused; light cancel, if used. Copies possessing all the above premium attributes are very difficult.

Caveats
Beware regumming and reperfing. Certificate optional.

24c CARMINE ROSE & BLUE
YEAR OF ISSUE: 1918
SCOTT NO. C3

Scarcity
Quantity Issued: 3,095,955
★ Average No./Auction: 1.44

Hinging
NH: 55.6%
Hinged: 44.4%

Comments
Although not small margined, this stamp is typically poorly centered as the examples on the right illustrate; the one on the left is a gem, the kind which is prized but seldom encountered. Nicely centered copies with large margins are prized, and difficult, especially never hinged. This stamp is often hinged, however, never hinged copies are not scarce. Most copies appearing at auction were never hinged. Natural gum skips are occasionally encountered and not considered a fault. Refer to the note on page 117 regarding natural inclusions.

Premium Characteristics
Sound condition, balanced margins (jumbo margined copies are worth a substantial premium), fresh color, never hinged (without gum skips), if unused; light cancel, if used. Copies possessing all the above premium attributes are very difficult.

Caveats
Beware regumming and reperfing. Certificate optional.

8c-24c AIRMAILS
YEAR OF ISSUE: 1923
SCOTT NO. C4-C6

Scarcity
Quantities Issued:

No. C4	(8c)	6,414,576
No. C5	(16c)	5,309,276
No. C6	(24c)	5,285,776

★ Avg No./Auction (C4):	.62
★ Avg No./Auction (C5):	1.48
★ Avg No./Auction (C6):	1.28

Hinging
No. C4 NH:	70.5%
No. C4 Hinged:	29.5%
No. C5 NH:	70.8%
No. C5 Hinged:	29.2%
No. C6 NH:	59.1%
No. C6 Hinged:	40.9%

General Comments
These stamps are typically poorly centered. The illustrated examples show a range of centering, with the poorly centered copies being more typical of the issue. These stamps are often hinged, however, never hinged copies are not scarce. Nicely centered copies with large margins are particularly prized, and difficult, especially never hinged. Most copies appearing at auction were never hinged. Natural gum skips are occasionally encountered and not considered a fault. Refer to the note on page 117 regarding natural inclusions.

Premium Characteristics
Sound condition, balanced margins (jumbo margined copies are worth a substantial premium), fresh color, never hinged (without gum skips), if unused; light cancel, if used. Copies possessing all the above premium attributes are very difficult.

Caveats
Regumming and reperfing occasionally encountered. Certificate optional.

10c DARK BLUE, BOOKLET PANE
YEAR OF ISSUE: 1927
SCOTT NO. C10a
Scarcity
Quantity Issued: 873,360
★ Average No./Auction: .53

Hinging
NH: 94.2%
Hinged: 5.8%

Comments
Centering is variable on this pane. The illustrated example is nicely margined and centered. Gum is usually never hinged. Hinged copies sell at a discount. Fakes exist, trimmed from sheet stamps with top selvedge.

Premium Characteristics
Sound condition, reasonable centering, fresh color, never hinged, if unused; light cancel, if used. Premium unused copies are not difficult. Complete used booklet panes are very scarce.

Caveats
Beware fake panes, which usually possess excessively narrow exterior margins. Avoid panes without full top selvedge.

GRAF ZEPPELIN ISSUE
YEAR OF ISSUE: 1930
SCOTT NOS. C13-C15

Scarcity
Quantity Issued:

No. C13	93,536
No. C14	72,428
No. C15	61,296

★ Avg No./Auction (C13):	1.74
⊙ Avg No./Auction (C13):	.32
★ Avg No./Auction (C14):	1.47
⊙ Avg No./Auction (C14):	.32
★ Avg No./Auction (C15):	1.23
⊙ Avg No./Auction (C15):	.10

Hinging

No. C13 NH:	55.2%
No. C13 Hinged:	44.8%
No. C14 NH:	48.6%
No. C14 Hinged:	51.4%
No. C15 NH:	53.3%
No. C15 Hinged:	46.7%

General Comments
Centering is variable on this issue; a wide range of grades exist. Nicely centered copies are not difficult, however of the three values, No. C14 seems to be the most difficult. The illustration shows some typical examples of C13-15 on the left; nicely centered copies appear on the right. Never hinged copies are abundant. Some copies contain natural gum skips. Natural gum bends are common, however, severe gum creases that affect the integrity of the paper should be avoided. Traces of guide lines on perforations is not an indication of reperforating; the Zeppelins were not issued with straight edges. However, occasionally reperforated copies (usually to improve centering) are seen.

Premium Characteristics
Sound condition, balanced margins, fresh color, never hinged (without gum skips), if unused; neat, non-obliterative cancel, if used. Premium copies possessing all the above attributes are moderately difficult. Finding sets of three, each with similar sized margins and centering, is more difficult than locating individually nice copies. Truly superb sets, with all three stamps similarly margined and centered and with post-office-fresh original gum free of bends, are very scarce and command a substantial premium.

Caveats
Beware regumming. Reperfing occasionally encountered. Certificate optional.

50c GREEN
YEAR OF ISSUE: 1933
SCOTT NO. C18

Scarcity
Quantity Issued: 4,302,950
★ Average No./Auction: 2.45
⊚ Average No./Auction: .29

Hinging
NH: 77.4%
Hinged: 22.6%

Comments
Typically well centered with poor copies the exception. Never hinged copies are abundant. Natural gum skips are occasionally encountered and not considered a fault. Natural gum bends are common. Regumming occasionally occurs but is really not a problem and can be spotted by comparing suspect gum with that of an inexpensive airmail of the same era.

Premium Characteristics
Sound condition, balanced margins, fresh color, never hinged (without gum skips), if unused; light cancel, if used. Premium copies possessing all the above attributes are not difficult.

Caveats
Beware regumming. Certificate optional.

10c BLUE
YEAR OF ISSUE: 1885
SCOTT NO. E1

Scarcity
Quantity Issued: 6,250,000 est.
★ Average No./Auction: 1.41

Hinging
NH: 9.8%
Hinged: 90.1%

Comments
This stamp is typically poorly centered. Centering characteristic of this issue can be seen on the illustrated block of four. The illustrated single is nicer than many.

Irregular perfs are frequently encountered and not considered a fault. Used copies are often heavily canceled. Faults are commonplace. Gum is usually heavily hinged or disturbed. Regumming and reperfing are often encountered.

Premium Characteristics
Sound condition, reasonably balanced margins, fresh color, lightly hinged or never hinged original gum, if unused. Premium unused copies are extremely difficult; premium used copies are difficult.

Caveats
Beware faults and repairs, including regumming and reperfing. Certificate recommended for never hinged.

10c BLUE
YEAR OF ISSUE: 1888
SCOTT NO. E2

Scarcity
Quantity Issued: not known
★ Average No./Auction: .34

Hinging
NH: 20.6%
Hinged: 79.4%

Comments
This stamp is typically poorly centered. Centering characteristic of this stamp can be seen on the illustrated block of four. Nicely centered copies are difficult. The illustrated single is very fine for this issue. Irregular perfs are frequently encountered and not considered a fault. Used copies are usually heavily canceled. Faults are commonplace. Gum is typically heavily hinged or disturbed. Regumming and reperfing are often encountered.

Premium Characteristics
Sound condition, reasonably balanced margins, fresh color, lightly hinged or never hinged original gum, if unused. Premium unused copies are extremely difficult.

Caveats
Beware faults and repairs, including regumming and reperfing. Certificate recommended for never hinged.

10c ORANGE
YEAR OF ISSUE: 1893
SCOTT NO. E3

Scarcity
Quantity Issued: 5,099,500
★ Average No./Auction: .64

Hinging
NH: 31.7%
Hinged: 68.3%

Comments
Basically the same stamp as No. E2 except for the color. Margins and centering characteristics similar to Nos. E1 and E2 (refer to illustrations with those listings). Nicely centered copies are difficult. The illustrated example is very fine for this issue. Color is susceptible to chemical change (browning). Irregular perfs are frequently encountered and not considered a fault. Used copies are usually heavily canceled. Faults are commonplace. Gum is typically heavily hinged or disturbed. Regumming and reperfing are often encountered. Paper and gum used for the this issue is the same as used for the Columbians.

Premium Characteristics
Sound condition, reasonably balanced margins, fresh color, lightly hinged or never hinged original gum, if unused. Premium unused copies are extremely difficult.

Caveats
Beware faults and repairs, including regumming and reperfing. Certificate recommended for never hinged.

10c BLUE
YEAR OF ISSUE: 1894
SCOTT NO. E4

Scarcity
Quantity Issued: not known
★ Average No./Auction: .72

Hinging
NH: 18.3%
Hinged: 81.7%

Comments
Exists in several shades. The stamp is typically poorly centered. Characteristic centering can be seen on the illustrated block of four. The single is a gem as nicely margined and centered as one could wish for. Irregular perfs are frequently encountered and not considered a fault. Gum is typically heavily hinged or disturbed. Regumming and reperfing are often encountered. Used copies are usually heavily canceled. Faults are commonplace.

Premium Characteristics
Sound condition, reasonably balanced margins, fresh color, lightly hinged or never hinged original gum, if unused. Premium unused copies are extremely difficult.

Caveats
Beware faults and repairs, including regumming and reperfing. Certificate recommended for never hinged.

10c ULTRAMARINE
YEAR OF ISSUE: 1916
SCOTT NO. E10

Scarcity
Quantity Issued: not known
★ Average No./Auction: .54

Hinging
NH: 53.5%
Hinged: 46.5%

Comments
This stamp often found with large margins, however, centering is typically poor. The block illustrates the variable nature of centering. Perfs are often rough, as typical for perf 10 stamps. Gum is typically hinged, often heavily. Regumming and reperfing are sometimes encountered. Used copies are frequently heavily canceled.

Premium Characteristics
Sound condition, reasonably balanced margins, fresh color, lightly hinged or never hinged original gum, if unused. Premium unused copies are extremely difficult.

Caveats
Beware faults and repairs, including regumming and reperfing. Beware fakes made from reperfed copies of large margined Scott No. E11. Certificate recommended for never hinged.

POSTAGE DUE SERIES OF 1879
COLOR: BROWN
SCOTT NOS. J1-J7

Scarcity
Quantities Issued:

No. J1	(1c)	16,000,000 est.
No. J2	(2c)	5,000,000 est.
No. J3	(3c)	30,000,000 est.
No. J4	(5c)	3,350,000 est.
No. J5	(10c)	3,250,000 est.
No. J6	(30c)	116,000 est.
No. J7	(50c)	85,000 est.

★ Avg No./Auction (J2):	.09
★ Avg No./Auction (J4):	.15
★ Avg No./Auction (J5):	.07
★ Avg No./Auction (J6):	.25
★ Avg No./Auction (J7):	.13

Note: Nos. J1 and J3 are of moderate value and were not surveyed, however, the same general condition comments apply to them.

Hinging

No. J2 NH:	33.3%
No. J4 NH:	46.7%
No. J5 NH:	0.0%
No. J6 NH:	8.0%
No. J7 NH:	7.7%

General Comments
Postage due stamps are much more elusive than their regular banknote counterparts. The 5-cent is the most difficult of the series, with few copies ever appearing at auction.

This series is small margined and typically poorly centered, as the illustrated examples show. The third from the left is an uncharacteristically large margined copy. Copies with balanced margins are very difficult. Irregular perfs are frequently encountered and not considered a fault. Gum is typically heavily hinged or disturbed. Never hinged copies are extremely scarce, especially for No. J5. Faults are commonplace. Regumming and reperfing are encountered frequently enough to be a problem. Used copies are often heavily canceled.

Premium Characteristics
Sound condition, reasonably balanced margins, good color, lightly hinged original gum, if unused; neat, attractive cancel, if used. Premium unused copies are exceedingly difficult.

Caveats
Beware faults and repairs, including regumming and reperfing. It is easy for the inexperienced eye to confuse this series with the later red-brown colored stamps of the same design. Certificate recommended for unused copies, and is essential never hinged.

POSTAGE DUE SERIES OF 1879
SPECIAL PRINTING OF 1880
SCOTT NOS. J8-J14

Scarcity
Quantity Issued:

No. J8	(1c)	4,420
No. J9	(2c)	1,361
No. J10	(3c)	436
No. J11	(5c)	249
No. J12	(10c)	174
No. J13	(30c)	179
No. J14	(50c)	170

★ Average No./Auction:

No. J8	.02
No. J9	.03
No. J10	.01
No. J11	.03
No. J12	.10
No. J13	.03
No. J14	.07

Comments
Issued on soft porous paper, both with and without gum. Typically poorly centered as the illustration shows. Often with faults, especially thins. Irregular perfs are typical and not considered a fault. These stamps (especially the low values) rarely appear at auction. Color is typically deep and rich, and impression clear and sharp. Seldom found with original gum and never hinged copies are virtually non-existent.

Premium Characteristics
The population is too small to permit selectivity in the normal sense.

Caveats
Beware faults and repairs. Certificate essential.

POSTAGE DUE SERIES OF 1884
COLOR: RED BROWN
SCOTT NOS. J15-J21

Scarcity
Quantities Issued: n/a

★ Avg No./Auction (J17): .04
★ Avg No./Auction (J18): .07
★ Avg No./Auction (J19): .08
★ Avg No./Auction (J20): .40
★ Avg No./Auction (J21): .16

Note: Nos. J15 and J16 are of moderate value and were not surveyed, however, the same general condition comments apply to them.

Hinging
Note: Too few copies appeared at auction to provide a valid sample, however, most copies are hinged; never hinged copies are rare, except for the 30-cent value, which for some reason, appears much more frequently at auction, and much more frequently in never hinged condition.

General Comments
Postage due stamps are much more elusive than their regular banknote counterparts, and this series is much scarcer than the either the 1879 or 1891 issue. These stamps are small margined and typically poorly centered. The illustrated examples are characteristic. Copies with balanced margins are very difficult. Gum is typically heavily hinged or disturbed. Faults are commonplace. Irregular perfs are frequently encountered and not considered a fault. Used copies are typically heavily canceled.

Premium Characteristics
Sound condition, reasonably balanced margins, good color, lightly hinged original gum, if unused; light cancel, if used. Premium unused copies are exceedingly difficult.

Caveats
Beware faults and repairs, including regumming and reperfing. It is easy for the inexperienced eye to confuse this series with the 1879 issue. Certificate recommended for unused copies, and is absolutely essential never hinged.

POSTAGE DUE SERIES OF 1891
COLOR: BRIGHT CLARET
SCOTT NOS. J22-J28

Scarcity
Quantities Issued: n/a

★ Avg No./Auction (J27): .08
★ Avg No./Auction (J28): .23

General Comments
Same general comments as for Nos. J15-J21. Centering and margin characteristics are similar. Of the three regularly issued large-format postage dues, this series is least difficult. Too few copies appeared at auction to provide a valid sample, however, most copies are hinged; never hinged copies are scarce.

Premium Characteristics
Sound condition, reasonably balanced margins, good color, lightly hinged original gum (never hinged copies exist but are very scarce), if unused; light cancel, if used. Premium unused copies are extremely difficult.

Caveats
Beware faults and repairs, including regumming and reperfing. Certificate recommended for unused copies, and is essential never hinged.

Comments
A very rare, very elusive stamp, typically small margined and poorly centered. The illustrated examples are very nice for this issue. Usually hinged, often heavily. Never hinged copies are extremely rare. Faults are commonplace.

1c VERMILION
YEAR OF ISSUE: 1894
SCOTT NO. J29

Scarcity
Quantity Issued: n/a
★ Average No./Auction: .08

Hinging
NH: 5.2%
Hinged: 94.8%

Premium Characteristics
Sound condition, reasonably balanced margins, fresh color, lightly hinged (or never hinged), if unused; light cancel, if used. Both unused and used premium copies are rare.

Caveats
Beware faults and repairs, including regumming and reperfing. Certificate essential.

2c VERMILION
YEAR OF ISSUE: 1894
SCOTT NO. J30

Scarcity
Quantity Issued: n/a
★ Average No./Auction: .09

Note: This stamp was not surveyed used.

Hinging
NH: 0.0%
Hinged:100.0%

Comments
A very elusive stamp, and like No. J29, typically small margined and poorly centered. The illustrated example is very nice for this issue. Gum is typically heavily hinged or disturbed. Never hinged copies are very rare. Faults are commonplace. Also very scarce used.

Premium Characteristics
Sound condition, reasonably balanced margins, fresh color, lightly hinged (or never hinged), if unused; light cancel, if used. Both unused and used premium copies are extremely difficult.

Caveats
Beware faults and repairs, including regumming and reperfing. Certificate essential.

POSTAGE DUE SERIES OF 1894-5
Perf 12, Unwatermarked
COLOR: DEEP CLARET
SCOTT NOS. J31-J37

Scarcity
Quantities Issued: n/a

★ Avg No./Auction (J34): .00
★ Avg No./Auction (J35): .00
★ Avg No./Auction (J36): .06
★ Avg No./Auction (J37): .10

Note: Nos. J31, J32, and J33 are of moderate value and were not surveyed, however, the same general condition comments apply to them. No copies of Nos. J34 or J35 appeared at auction in the survey.

Hinging
Note: Too few copies appeared at auction to provide a valid sample, however, it is known that never hinged copies of Nos. J34-J37 are rare.

General Comments
Except for the low values of the group, this series is one of the most difficult of the postage dues. Unused upper values seldom appear at auction, and when they do, they are typically faulty. The stamps are small margined and usually poorly centered. Characteristic margins and centering are shown on the illustrated blocks. Copies with balanced margins are very difficult. Gum is typically heavily hinged or disturbed. Used copies are frequently heavily canceled. The 30-cent value exists in a pale rose shade, which is less scarce than the deep claret.

Premium Characteristics
Sound condition, reasonably balanced margins, fresh color, lightly hinged or never hinged original gum, if unused; light cancel, if used. Premium unused copies are exceedingly difficult.

Caveats
Beware faults and repairs, including regumming and reperfing. Certificate recommended for unused copies, and is absolutely essential never hinged gum.

POSTAGE DUE SERIES OF 1895-7
Perf 12, Double Line Watermark
COLOR: DEEP CLARET
SCOTT NOS. J38-J44

Scarcity
Quantities Issued: n/a

★ Avg No./Auction (J43): .09
★ Avg No./Auction (J33): .12

General Comments
Unused upper values seldom appear at auction, and when they do, they are typically faulty. They share the same centering and margin characteristics as Nos. J31-J37 above (see illustration). Copies with balanced margins are very difficult. Gum is typically heavily hinged or disturbed. Never hinged copies of J43-J44 are rare. Used copies are frequently heavily canceled.

Premium Characteristics
Sound condition, reasonably balanced margins, good color, lightly hinged or never hinged original gum, if unused; light cancel, if used. Premium unused copies of the lower values are difficult; the upper values are exceedingly difficult.

Caveats
Beware faults and repairs, including regumming and reperfing. Certificate recommended for unused copies, and is absolutely essential never hinged gum.

POSTAGE DUE SERIES OF 1910-12
Perf 12, Single Line Watermark
COLOR: DEEP CLARET
SCOTT NOS. J45-J50

Scarcity
Quantities Issued: n/a

★ Avg No./Auction (J47):   .08
★ Avg No./Auction (J50):   .07

Note: Nos. J45, J46, J48, and J49 are of moderate value and were not surveyed, however, the same general condition comments apply to them.

Hinging
Note: Too few copies appeared at auction to provide a valid sample, however, it is known that never hinged copies of Nos. J47-J50 are rare.

General Comments
These share the same centering and margin characteristics as Nos. J31-J44 (refer to the illustration above Nos. J31-J37). Copies with balanced margins are scarce. Gum is typically heavily hinged or disturbed. The upper values seldom appear at auction, and when they do, they are typically faulty. Used copies are frequently heavily canceled.

Premium Characteristics
Sound condition, reasonably balanced margins, good color, lightly hinged or never hinged original gum, if unused; light cancel, if used. Premium unused copies are difficult; premium unused copies of Nos. J47 and J50 are exceedingly difficult.

Caveats
Beware faults and repairs, including regumming and reperfing. Certificate recommended for unused copies of the more expensive values, and is absolutely essential for NH copies of those values.

POSTAGE DUE SERIES OF 1914
Perf 10, Single Line Watermark
COLOR: CARMINE LAKE
SCOTT NOS. J52-J58

Scarcity
Quantities Issued: n/a

★ Avg No./Auction (J57):   .29
★ Avg No./Auction (J58):   .06

Note: Nos. J52-J56 are of moderate value and were not surveyed, however, the same general condition comments apply to them.

Hinging
Note: Too few copies appeared at auction to provide a valid sample, however, it is known that never hinged copies of No. J57 are scarce; never hinged copies of No. J58, if they exist, are exceedingly rare.

General Comments
Unused upper values seldom appear at auction, and when they do, they are typically faulty. Irregular perfs are to be expected on this issue, as is usual for perf 10s. The stamps are usually poorly centered, especially Scott No. J58, which is so scarce that even moderately well centered copies seldom appear. Copies with balanced margins are very difficult. The illustrated examples show characteristic centering and margins of this issue. Gum is typically heavily hinged or disturbed. Used copies are usually heavily canceled.

Premium Characteristics
Sound condition, reasonably balanced margins, good color, lightly hinged (or never hinged) original gum, if unused; light cancel, if used. Premium unused copies of the lower values are difficult; premium copies of No. J57 are extremely difficult. No. J58 is rare in any form, and virtually non-existent in premium condition.

Caveats
Beware faults and repairs, including regumming and reperfing. Certificate strongly recommended for unused copies, and is absolutely essential for NH.

1c ROSE, Perf 10, Unwatermarked
YEAR OF ISSUE: 1916
SCOTT NO. J59

Scarcity
Quantity Issued: n/a
★ Average No./Auction: .06
⊙ Average No./Auction: .03

Comments
A very elusive stamp, typically poorly centered. Horizontal spacing between stamps is narrow; therefore, copies with balanced margins are difficult, as can be seen in the illustration. Perfs are usually irregular and often rough, as is the case with all perf 10s, and not considered a

fault. Note the perfs in the illustration. Gum is usually hinged, often heavily. Never hinged copies, if they exist, are exceedingly rare (none were encountered in the survey). Faults are commonplace.

Premium Characteristics
Sound condition, reasonably balanced margins, fresh color, lightly hinged (or never hinged), if unused; light cancel, if used. Premium copies are rare.

Caveats
Beware faults and repairs, including regumming and reperfing. Certificate essential.

2c ROSE, Perf 10, Unwatermarked
YEAR OF ISSUE: 1916
SCOTT NO. J60

Scarcity
Quantity Issued: n/a
★ Average No./Auction: .09

Comments
A very elusive stamp, which appears at auction much less frequently than its moderate catalogue value would suggest. The general comments for No. J59 also apply to this stamp. Gum is typically heavily hinged or disturbed. Never hinged

copies are very rare. Faults are commonplace.

Premium Characteristics
Sound condition, reasonably balanced margins, fresh color, lightly hinged (or never hinged), if unused; light cancel, if used. Premium copies are extremely difficult.

Caveats
Beware faults and repairs, including regumming and reperfing. Certificate recommended, especially for never hinged.

SHANGHAI SET
YEAR OF ISSUE: 1919
SCOTT NOS. K1-K16

Scarcity
Quantities Issued: n/a

★ Avg No./Auction (K15):   .48
★ Avg No./Auction (K16):   .75

Note: Neither lower values nor used copies were surveyed.

Hinging
NH (K15):   14.3%
NH (K16):   20.3%

General Comments
These stamps are typically poorly centered as is usual for Washington-Franklins. The illustrated examples show the variation in centering that can be expected. Gum is typically hinged. When purchased as a complete set, it is almost impossible to find stamps uniformly very fine throughout. These stamps were on sale at the Philatelic Agency in Washington, DC, for an extended period of time, and, therefore, are much more abundant unused than legitimately used. Never hinged copies of the less expensive stamps are not scarce; never hinged higher values are somewhat more difficult.

Premium Characteristics
Sound condition, reasonably balanced margins, fresh color, never hinged, if unused; neat, appropriate cancel, if used. Premium copies of the lower values are not terribly difficult; the higher values are more elusive.

Caveats
Beware faults and repairs, including regumming and reperfing. Certificate recommended for used copies on cover and never hinged high values.

PARCEL POST SERIES
YEAR OF ISSUE: 1913
SCOTT NOS. Q1-Q12

Scarcity
Quantities Issued:

No. Q1	(1c)	209,691,094
No. Q2	(2c)	206,417,253
No. Q3	(3c)	29,027,433
No. Q4	(4c)	76,743,813
No. Q5	(5c)	108,153,993
No. Q6	(10c)	56,896,653
No. Q7	(15c)	21,147,033
No. Q8	(20c)	17,142,393
No. Q9	(25c)	21,940,653
No. Q10	(50c)	2,117,793
No. Q11	(75c)	2,772,615
No. Q12	($1)	1,053,273

★ Avg No./Auction (Q10): .55
★ Avg No./Auction (Q12): .65

Note: Neither lower values of this set nor used copies were surveyed.

Hinging
NH (Q10): 22.2%
NH (Q12): 25.0%

General Comments
These stamps are large margined and typically much better centered than other stamps of the era. Of the group, the 15-, 20-, and 25-cent values are surprisingly difficult to find well centered and with generous margins. The stamps on the top row show just how nicely margined and centered this issue can be; those on the bottom row show centering more typical of the issue. Gum is usually hinged, however, never hinged copies of the less expensive stamps are not scarce; the higher values are more difficult. Keep an eye open for reperfing and regumming on unused copies.

Premium Characteristics
Sound condition, balanced margins (jumbo margined copies are worth a substantial premium), fresh color, never hinged, if unused; light cancel, if used. Premium copies of the less expensive stamps are not difficult (the 15-, 20-, and 25-cents values are the most troublesome of the group); premium copies of the keys (Nos. Q10 & Q12) are only moderately difficult.

Caveats
Beware faults and repairs, including regumming and reperfing. Certificate recommended only for more expensive premium never hinged copies.

PARCEL POST DUE SERIES
YEAR OF ISSUE: 1912
SCOTT NOS. JQ1-JQ5

Scarcity
Quantities Issued:

No. JQ1	(1c)	7,322,400
No. JQ2	(2c)	3,132,000
No. JQ3	(5c)	5,840,100
No. JQ4	(10c)	2,124,540
No. JQ5	(25c)	2,117,700

★ Avg No./Auction (JQ4):   .27

Note: Only No. JQ4, the most expensive value of the set was surveyed unused; none were surveyed used.

Hinging
NH (JQ4):   16.8%

General Comments
Although margined similarly to the parcel posts, the parcel post dues seem to be more difficult to find well centered. The illustrated block shows centering typical of the issue. The single examples are fairly nice for this issue. Parcel post dues are usually hinged, however, never hinged copies of the less expensive stamps are not scarce; Scott Nos. JQ4 and JQ5 are somewhat more difficult, but not rare. Keep an eye open for reperfing and regumming on unused copies. Irregular perfs are frequently encountered and not considered a fault.

Premium Characteristics
Sound condition, balanced margins (jumbo margined copies are worth a substantial premium), fresh color, never hinged, if unused; light cancel, if used. Premium copies of Scott Nos. JQ1 and JQ3 are not difficult; premium copies of the others (Scott Nos. JQ2, JQ4 & JQ5) are more difficult.

Caveats
Beware faults and repairs, including regumming and reperfing. Certificate recommended for copies on cover.

BIBLIOGRAPHY

Brookman, Lester G., *The Postage Stamps of the Nineteenth Century*, three volumes, David G. Phillips Publishing Co., 1989.

Johl, Max G., *United States Postage Stamps 1902-1935*, Quartermain Publications, 1976.

Luff, John M., *The Postage Stamps of the United States*, Scott Stamp & Coin Company, 1937.

Michel USA Spezial Katalog 1989, Schwaneberger Verlag GMBH, 1989.

Minkus New American Stamp Catalog- 1982, Minkus Publications, 1982.

Postage Stamps of the United States 1847-1961. U.S. Government Printing Office, 1962.

Schmid, Paul, *The Expert's Book*, Palm Press, 1990.

Scott Specialized Catalogue of United States Stamps - 1992, Scott Publishing Co., 1991.

White, R.H., *Encyclopedia of the Colors of United States Postage Stamps*, *Vols. I-IV*, Philatelic Research Ltd, 1981.

AUCTION BIBLIOGRAPHY

Earl P.L. Apfelbaum, Inc.
Aubrey Bartlett, Inc.
Matthew Bennett, Inc.
William A. Fox, Inc.
Harmers of New York, Inc.
Sam Houston Philatelic, Inc.
Daniel F. Kelleher, Inc.
Robert E. Lippert

Ivy, Shreve & Mader, Inc.
Greg Manning, Inc.
Rasdale Stamp Co.
Satuit Philatelics Corp.
Jacques Schiff, Jr., Inc.
Robert A. Siegel, Inc.
Superior Galleries, Inc.
Richard Wolffers, Inc.